AN UNFORGETTABLE VISIT TO AFRICA...

KENYA'S MASAI MARA GAME RESERVE . . . *John Heminway takes a "short walk" through the land of the Masai to discover the true nature of their exotic culture. If you would like to see Africa on foot, he recommends a camel safari in Kenya's north: They carry the supplies while you walk with guide Simon Evans over the beautiful terrain, viewing the desert animals and meeting Samburu tribesmen.*

"THE IRON SNAKE" . . . *Heminway drinks champagne and travels like a pasha on the Nairobi–Mombasa train line, and you can enjoy the "absolute African extravaganza" as you get a taste of old-style train travel complete with dinner served on china and linen in the dining car.*

THE CHOBE GAME LODGE . . . *Heminway gives away a brilliantly kept secret when he describes his stay at the edge of the Kalahari Desert, where at cocktail hour, battle-scarred hippos lunge and yawn, preparing for night-time forays on this luxurious hotel's lawn.*

GOMBE . . . *This is the site of Jane Goodall's famous study of primates, and Heminway not only introduces the reader to the feisty, dedicated Ms. Goodall, but tells you how to journey there for a three-day visit with the chimps and how to continue your vacation to the Zaire/Rwanda border and an encounter with the mountain gorillas.*

AMBOSELI . . . *One of Heminway's deepest passions is for the elephant, and here he describes the grave threat that is fast depleting their numbers, while he holds us spellbound with elephant stories. You can go elephant watching, too, in Amboseli, Kenya, or to truly out-of-the-way reserves in Zambia and Zimbabwe.*

GIRAFFE NEAR KITICH, NORTHERN KENYA

also by the author

NO MAN'S LAND
THE IMMINENT RAINS

AFRICAN JOURNEYS

A Personal Guidebook

JOHN HEMINWAY

WARNER BOOKS

A Warner Communications Company

Warner Books, Inc., 666 Fifth Avenue, New York, NY 10103

w A Warner Communications Company

Printed in the United States of America
First printing: September 1990
10 9 8 7 6 5 4 3 2 1

Library of Congress Cataloging-in-Publication Data

Heminway, John Hylan, 1944–
  African journeys : a personal guidebook / John Heminway.
    p.   cm.
  ISBN 0-446-38795-9
  1. Africa—Description and travel—1977——Guide-books.
I. Title
DT2.H45   1990
916.04'329—dc20   90-12152
                                                     CIP

BOOK DESIGN BY SIGNET M DESIGN, INC.

All photos courtesy of John Heminway.
"Serengeti Shall Not Die"
From Smithsonian magazine, February 1987
"Tomorrow I Plan to Go for a Walk"
GEO Special on East Africa, November 20, 1989
"The Romantic Hotels of Africa"
Connoisseur, August 1987
"An American Family's Unusual Christmas Safari"
© Town & Country magazine, The Hearst Corporation, December 1988
"The African Queen of Hotels: Kenya's Legendary Norfolk"
© Town & Country magazine, The Hearst Corporation, October 1986
"The Secret Coast"
This article was first published in the Condé Nast Traveler, November 1988.
"Traipsing Through Time"
This article was first published in the Condé Nast Traveler, November 1988.
"Elephant Voices"
This article was first published in the Condé Nast Traveler, February 1990.

To the
African Wildlife Foundation

ACKNOWLEDGMENTS

All my books have been formed out of friendships: chums have made contacts, provided inspiration, given me leads. A dusty-road encounter has led to a life-long association. My professional life, it would seem, is merely the polished exposure of a private world. Readers should therefore not be surprised to learn that the following essays represent a tangle of personal debts.

Rachel Wilder Smeragliuolo has contributed not only a golden retriever to my life but also the lion's share of the research and the writing of the "travel advisories." I am in her debt.

Others have been generous with their time and ideas and company in Africa. In particular I want to single out friends Mark Stanley Price, Geoff and Jorie Kent, Sven Lindblad, John and Angela Sutton, Sandy Evans, Annie Vincent, Peter Jones, John Stevens and Jonathan Kenworthy. Kathy Eldon helped me with Kenyan restaurant advice. Best of all, Dita Amory once sacrificed a holiday and most of her weekends to this book—an act of selflessness I will not forget.

My splendid agent, Jacques de Spoelberch, fought tenaciously for African Journeys. So too did Susan Suffes, a very careful and caring editor who, incredibly, survived my stormy moods. Martin Rapp, Candy Olmstead and Jane Grossman of the Travellers Bookstore represent the force that launched and sustained this book from flimsy notion to commissioned concept. I am grateful.

Of all my distinguished colleagues at the African Wildlife Foundation, Diana McMeekin deserves special thanks for the considerable time she devoted to answering Rachel's and my questions. My fellow trustee Leslee Dart supplied many updates.

Thanks also to Harry Evans, Maggy Simmons and Kathy Kelley for supporting a strand of African articles at Condé Nast Traveler.

Finally, my special thanks to four very talented associates at Channel

Thirteen——Chelle Tutt, Sarah Wood, Laura Trust, and Marion Swaybill. They gave me the time, the support and the confidence that allowed me to finish writing in the midst of a demanding broadcast schedule.

In a book filled with so many details there are bound to be oversights, inconsistencies and errors. No one but me should be blamed.

CONTENTS

Baobab in Tarangire National Park, Tanzania

AN INTRODUCTION:

First African Footsteps

I FIRST SIGHTED AFRICA FROM THE PLUNG-
ing fo'castle of a mailship called the *Winchester Castle*. I was sixteen
and had originally hoped to spend the summer in Alaska, but when
I saw dawn turn Table Mountain first to purple, then to tarnished
sable, my heart skipped. Even then I knew things had changed
forever.

My heart skips today. Those great Cape rollers had washed me
ashore on an unresolved headland. Whisper "Africa" to me now,
nearly thirty years later, and still I smell dust and wood smoke
and sweet sweat, I hear an emerald-spotted wood dove, I feel the
evening breeze rising from the plains, drying my skin here on the
crest of a hill; before me I see not just the distance but a link
between time and space, folding in upon itself, wave after wave
of prismatic heat, punctuated by a hollow horizon far away.

I haven't yet uncovered all secrets in green hills, faded plains,
yellowed riverbeds. Zebra and buffalo meandering below me heading for the water hole are proof positive of my ignorance. So, too,
those elephants I nearly mistook for boulders. And the goat bells
accompanied by a whoop of long-distance chatter reassure me that
here in the amplitude of a barren land I am never altogether alone.

As soon as I was beached in Africa I found what I had lacked
in myself. Thus, drowned in dust, whiplashed by heat, scared sick
by lions, I learned I was far from complete. I saw that souls and
not just bodies suffer and adjust and swell in a sequence not
dissimilar from Darwin's Laws of Natural Selection. Because of
Africa I came to accept that I would always be on the drawing

boards, forever thirsty on a plain that reaches for the Southern Cross.

Fair enough: Man was born in Africa. No doubt I'm happy to be home. But there is more to this wrenching continent than anatomical atavism. There is soul talk in the silence, stomach wails at dawn, gibberish of the larynx during that loneliest hour of the night. Africa has become for me, now middle-aged I suppose, a womb of questions, its smoky air just before the rains the amniotic fluid of self-doubt.

I must say I am not troubled by feeling small and lost and thirsty for a home in the Africa I carry around in my head. To me, hell is assuming all the answers. Today, I still stumble to understand myself amid the peculiar set of references I started finding in Africa at age sixteen. Amid all this floundering my heart will skip another beat. Talk about homesickness! These days I'm soulsick from absence long before I ever leave Africa.

With feelings such as these it should be no surprise I have become a missionary for my cherished continent. I believe there is no sickness of the heart too great it cannot be cured by a dose of Africa. Families must go there to learn why they belong together on this earth, adolescents to discover humility, lovers to plumb old but untried wells of passion, honeymooners to seal marriages with a shared sense of bafflement, those shopworn with life to find a tonic for futility, the aged to recognize a symmetry to twilight. I know this all sounds a bit much, but if ever I have seen magic, it has been in Africa.

Of course Africa only cures the curable. I have had my failures—the restaurant guide-writer who returned to New York and said the landscapes were underwhelming, the globetrotter from Palm Beach who was disappointed by the cooking, the black man from Cincinnati who said he counted his days in malaria pills.

Now I practice triage. No doubt abandoning the incurable and concentrating on the easy cases sounds insensitive, but there is no longer as much Africa to go around as there was when I was sixteen. I am relentlessly being asked by friends how to "do" Africa.

Invariably I begin not with advice but with questions: Why do you want to go to Africa? What do you hope to get out of Africa? What was the best holiday you ever had? The worst? Generally, I can spot those whom Africa will move. For them I gladly volunteer itineraries, the names of outfitting firms and guides, and practical reassurance about health, diet, and wardrobe.

But not everyone seems a perfect candidate. There are others for whom the Third World, tents, bugs, unscheduled rains, and a broken gearbox will be neither an adventure nor a laugh. No insult intended—some people do not *need* Africa. And in certain of their cases, I count them fortunate—they have been spared both heartache and expense. For them, a theme park like Lion Country Safari in Florida may do.

I have concocted this book along the lines of the advice I give my friends. Over the years I have offered specific and very personal recommendations for those intent on traveling to Kenya, Tanzania, Zambia, Zimbabwe, or Botswana. Then I have urged them to read book after book about Africa so that their trip will not merely be a succession of stops along a circular route but an itinerary with a heart. In this book, after specific advice for East and South Central Africa, I humbly offer my own enthusiasms, each related to destinations, safaris, and quarry in the regions specified.

So how can a reader know, at a flash, whether or not he or she is destined for the Serengeti or for Lion Country Safari? The test, I believe, is simple. First, there is the awkward matter of money. While there may be very inexpensive ways to see Africa—hitchhiking and using public transportation—I am not the appropriate authority on those. Anyone wishing to see Africa in the manner I specify should be willing to part with anywhere from $1000 or more (much more for first class) on round-trip airfare and then upward of $150 a day per person ($250 a day is more like it) on internal travel and subsistence.

The other, less vulgar test requires answering the following questions in the affirmative:

1. Am I affected by the knowledge that this earth's wildlife and wild lands are being depleted at a hideous rate?

2. Am I upset to hear that there are unchecked threats to those regions of Africa where so many of these wild lives and wild lands are to be found?

3. Can I remember recently being surprised, even shocked (a) by a discovery, (b) by a self-discovery?

4. Do I get along with members of other races, other cultures?

5. Would I prefer to learn something substantive about wildlife rather than merely wish to see every animal available on a checklist?

6. Do I remain in control in the presence of insects?

7. Am I capable of laughing when things go wrong?

If you can unequivocally answer "yes" to each of the above, an African safari is for you. The advisory sections of this book will now serve as a menu for initial conversations with your travel agent.

In these discussions, bear in mind that the choice of a guide is fundamental to the success of a safari. Somebody with character, charm, and real insight will spellbind. Since many safari guides visit Britain and the United States each year, you may be able to eliminate any doubt about the human chemistry of your vacation well in advance. If, however, you are unable to meet your guide in advance, barrage your travel agent with leading questions about character. Never be satisfied if his or her identity is not revealed. Be irate if one guide is promised and another delivered. A good guide will turn bad luck into laughter. Even if your Land Rover becomes mired in mud or the tents collapse during a high wind or the cook gets drunk one night, you will leave Africa euphoric. Success, I have discovered, depends first on personalities, second on food and comforts, last on wildlife. Game may be scarce, the weather rotten, your reception in a national park far from welcoming—these may not compromise the success of your safari. The choice of your guide will be the most important move you can make. In the end, it's a decision not worth squandering. Africa

LION IN KENYA'S MASAI MARA

is not Europe or Florida. Think of Africa as a place that you may only be allowed to visit once.

Perhaps this small book will help guide you through this continent where a sixteen-year-old once was beached, where he discovered a paradox in his life, where he grew young from enthusiasm. I wish you the same good fortune.

A D V I S O R Y

Where in Africa?

For so many, Africa looms as a monolithic mass with little interior definition. East and Central Africa are one contiguous whole, resounding with the hoofbeats of animals, very foreign, fairly inscrutable. For those unfamiliar with the lay of the land, a plain in Kenya could not be much different from one in Botswana, which surely must be a variant of Zambia. Right?

No. Each African country has a distinct character and will appeal to a specific set of safari dreams. There is no sense embarking for Kenya merely because it is the country highlighted in most travel brochures. There may easily be other destinations with more appeal. Here, therefore, is a thumbnail sketch of each.

K E N Y A • This is a country of immediate gratification: You want to see a lion, you will see a lion. Should you wish to lose your heart to a great mountain, camp in the highlands, see colossal migrations, dry out in the desert, luxuriate on a tropical beach, be treated to sumptuous meals, and live in near-regal splendor, you can. Just whistle. But there are liabilities to Kenya: You will face an almost insurmountable task in avoiding other travelers; native Kenyans can at times be spoiled,

money-hungry, off-hand; the general urban population suffers lamentable poverty; and poaching—particularly the poaching of rhino and elephant—is an ever-present blight on the land.

Having said the above, I would strongly urge a prospective traveler to Kenya to build an itinerary that is not exclusively centered on the Masai Mara, Amboseli, and the Mount Kenya Safari Club. This book will suggest great stretches of this beautiful land where tourists rarely venture.

TANZANIA •

Until a few years ago, Tanzania was where the intrepid went. The roads were appalling, the accommodations spartan, and the local attitude to tourism aloof at best. Today the official line has been reversed, to the benefit of the traveler.

Still, Tanzania is a country lacking the lavish frills of Kenya. Here the food is, as a rule, merely acceptable, the roads sometimes uncomfortable, the accommodations often lamentable. One goes to Tanzania for other reasons: for wonders of this world, such as the Serengeti migration, the Ngorongoro Crater, the Selous, unself-conscious Masai, unopposed hunter-gatherers. Wherever one travels in Tanzania, crowds are thinner than in Kenya. And the farther one departs the so-called milk run (Seronera, the Crater, and Lake Manyara), the greater the likelihood of being totally alone. Only for those who can afford a private camp and personal safari guide is Tanzania as luxurious as Kenya. In Africa, like everywhere else, the greatest of all luxuries is, of course, privacy.

ZAMBIA •

Here is a country with few people, hardly any mountains, an embattled capital, and pockets of wild land where one can dream one is the only person on the face of this earth. Many game-viewing areas, such as the Kafue Flats and the Bangweulu Swamps, are for specialists.

I propose one consider Zambia for only one reason at present: the Luangwa Valley. It consists of two noncontiguous wilderness areas, both quite flat, both veined by seasonal river systems, and both filled with game and birdlife (although sadly, as in most of Africa, poachers have more or less eliminated the rhino and have significantly reduced elephant numbers). Here tented camps are smaller than in East Africa (20 beds are the norm). Often they face inward to a campfire, as if "laagered" against nature. Game-viewing is conducted both on foot and in open Land Rovers, and the quality of guiding is without peer in Africa.

One should be careful when visiting Zambia to avoid any protracted stay in the charmless capital, Lusaka, since it is rife with crime and AIDS. The Luangwa Valley resembles a neat and prosperous pseudo-colonial outpost in the midst of a turbulent, economically unstable land.

ZIMBABWE • Most travelers are drawn here by

the sight of Victoria Falls. While stunning and romantic (far more than Niagara Falls), it has become a bit of a tourist trap and should be considered worthy of no more than two safari days. Guiding standards throughout this country are exceptionally high. Harare is a modern, comfortable city with good restaurants, reasonable shopping, and a large concentration of whites. There are a few historic sites near here, worthy of a day's outing.

Apart from the Falls, the country's greatest draw is the Zambezi watershed, where much of the country's wildlife is concentrated. Wilderness safaris, by foot or in canoe, are *de rigueur*—ideal for small family groups and a wonderful way to get on a first-name basis with the game. Here the half-dozen permanent camps are small and personalized. Generally they look out at the river, framed by Africa's lateral rift, olive gray and, on most evenings, heart-racing.

BOTSWANA • Almost all the country overlies

Kalahari sands. In the south, these are exposed as desert. In much of the north they have been swept by an extraordinary inland delta called the Okavango, which is unique in Africa, if not the world. Bird life is hugely concentrated, wildlife is quite rich, the patient observer is rewarded, and the setting is quintessentially Pleistocene. There are around 40 camps scattered throughout the Delta, each invisible to the other and each reached most efficiently by small aircraft. Game-viewing is often an early morning, late afternoon venture accomplished in a canoe, outboard, or occasionally by Land Rover. Camps, composed of tents or airy grass huts, are small and comfortable, serving good wines and delicious food. A week in the Delta should be divided between two or

possibly three camps, each complementing the other. As preface or epilog to the Delta, one should try to commit about two days to the Chobe River in the north. This is a narrow riverine habitat, part of the greater Zambezi system. It is pregnant with elephants, sable, crocs, and hippos and is a magnificent "bookend" to the Delta.

In Africa, there is no reason one's safari should not be split between countries. Much of the game and many of the birds are unique to a region. Safari styles vary. Perspectives are highly localized. Knowledge only of the Delta, the Serengeti, or the Luangwa will skew one's view of Africa. Instead, I recommend a safari to include opposites—cold highlands, steamy river bottoms, great water, dusty plains.

There is, of course, a drawback. Travel between African countries (even, sometimes, within an African nation) is sweaty, time-consuming business. A full day devoted to local airline schedules can be fairly demoralizing. Sometimes one must overnight in places of little moment—Dar es Salaam, Kariba, Lusaka, to be specific—which seem, at first glance, a thorough waste of time and money. On the other hand, you will discover that in Africa the getting there is always worthy of the destination. And, anyway, if you stop in an African capital like Dar es Salaam, where tourists are rare, you're bound to have an adventure you'll never forget.

A D V I S O R Y
Why Tents?

Tented camps are a relatively new development on the game-viewing scene in East Africa and Botswana. Until twenty years ago permanent lodges, like Keekorok in the Masai Mara or Kilaguni in Tsavo West, were small and comfortable; generally they provided the sole accommodations in national parks. They were operated personally—the lodge manager, who was everyone's friend, often

THE BEST TIME TO GO:
WEATHER AND GAME-VIEWING CHART

KEY: The best time *   Not bad 0   Don't bother X

Country	Location	Jan	Feb	Mar	Apr	May	Jun	Jul	Aug	Sep	Oct	Nov	Dec
KENYA													
	Amboseli	*	*	*	0	0	0	*	*	*	*	0	0
	Masai Mara	*	*	*	0	0	0	*	*	*	*	0	0
	Meru	*	*	*	0	X	0	*	*	*	*	0	0
	Samburu	*	*	*	0	X	0	*	*	*	*	0	0
	Tsavo	*	*	*	0	X	0	*	*	*	*	0	0
	Coast	*	*	0	X	X	X	0	0	0	*	*	*
TANZANIA													
	Lake Manyara and Ngorongoro Crater	*	*	*	0	0	*	*	*	*	*	0	0
	Serengeti	*	*	*	*	*	*	0	0	0	0	*	*
	Selous	0	0	0	X	X	0	*	*	*	0	X	0
	Tarangire	0	0	0	0	X	*	*	*	*	*	0	0
	Kilimanjaro	*	*	0	X	X	0	0	0	*	*	0	0
ZAMBIA													
	South Luangwa	*	*	*	*	*	0	*	*	*	0	X	X
ZIMBABWE													
	Mana Pools	X	X	X	X	X	0	*	*	*	*	X	X
BOTSWANA													
	Chobe and Okavango Delta	X	X	X	X	0	0	*	*	*	0	X	X

SERENGETI CAMP, TANZANIA

bought a round of drinks and performed pantomimes for your companions after hours around the bar. Dehumanized mass tourism was yet to overwhelm Africa.

Ever since Teddy Roosevelt's epic safari in 1909, the big game-hunting industry has been perfecting the design of tents. Those used in the early years were never of the small, lightweight variety common among backpackers in the United States and Britain. Made of heavy-duty canvas, supported by colossal poles, secured by long guy ropes and stout tent pegs, the classic "Manyara" tent, designed by Low and Bonar in Nairobi, provided hunting clients with all the comforts they could ever expect in the African bush—relative coolness in hot weather and safety from predators, snakes, and insects, as well as munificent roominess. For every tent there was one staff member whose sole job was to bring tea in the morning, iron your sheets during the day, and hoist a canvas bag filled with 102-degree water for your shower before your sundowner, or cocktail, beside the fire.

Professional hunter Glen Cottar was the first to see that the sybaritic hunters' camp could be modified to suit game viewers. I first met him in the mid-sixties, shortly after he had launched Tsavo Tsafaris, the fountainhead tented camp. With his Van Dyke beard, Glen became my definition of the Kenya swashbuckler. Gregarious and high-spirited, indifferent to the niceties of economics, continuously shadowed by a welter of equally high-spirited sons and friends of sons, he seemed hell-bent on risking life, limb, and bank account for his dreams. At the time, many of his fellow hunters thought him slightly touched to build a camp in a remote corner of Tsavo National Park for the benefit of a flaky breed of travelers notoriously wary of sleeping in tents. But Glen was never bothered by criticism.

The site Glen chose for Tsavo Tsafaris was on the northern bank of the Tsavo River, running through Tsavo East National Park. Road access was across thirty miles of hideous bush track. The final leg was by rubber boat. Often the Tsavo was in flood. As I recall, the first tents for the camp were travel-stained rejects from

his hunting business (no tourist ever caught on to this legerdemain). Laid out with military precision, each tent verandah commanded a knee-wobbling view of the river. In addition, Glen provided a large tent for a dining room and bar where one could repair in bad weather. Most evenings, one took one's meals around the fire, listening to the gush of the river.

I first saw the camp late one October afternoon some twenty-three years ago, when the Tsavo was in full flood. MaryAnne Richdale, my companion, and I spotted one white man and several blacks gesticulating from the far side of the river. Soon a flimsy rubber raft was launched. It bounced and skittered precariously until its skipper, the solitary white, was able to throw us a line. Dispensing with greetings, we clambered aboard and gamely hung on for the return journey, praying our cameras would not be dunked. Safely arrived at the far side, we watched our cases being carried by the liveried tent staff as we made our way to the campfire and a crisp Tusker beer.

Our host was Alan Price, the lonely camp manager. Because this was the low season, we were his only guests. MaryAnne and I may as well have been in our own camp. As soon as we had changed into *kikois* (a kind of sarong) for dinner, Alan launched into a litany of jokes and stories, each executed with a brilliant ear for dialect. I retired at midnight with a stomachache from the laughter, but MaryAnne stayed by the campfire until dawn to hear more. Sporadically during the night, I awoke to catch a question such as, "Have you heard the one about Babu, the stationmaster?" The response was rarely MaryAnne's; instead it blew in from the darkness—a rhino snorting in thick bush, hippos susurring in the river, a hoarse lion broadcasting his right of eminent domain. A tent, I discovered, was the perfect listening device for the African night. Here I might meet the wild in a delicate balance with civilization. Here all creatures, great and low, seemed to share the same solemn liturgy.

I have stayed in many tented camps since then. In each I feel like an insider to Africa. My corollary goes like this: Lodges are for tourists, tents for proper travelers. Today Glen Cottar's wild-eyed scheme has been appropriated everywhere throughout Kenya—even on coastal beaches. In Tanzania the development of tented camps is being resurrected after that nation's decade of xenophobia. Even in the Okavango Delta of Botswana, tented camps have proliferated.

Travelers in the know have now come to realize that a tent in Africa is no compromise to luxury. Indeed, some are equipped with cement foundations, rare Persian carpets, flush plumbing, and antique beds. Frankly, I find too much luxury intrusive, since the object of tenting is not to be a pampered pasha, but at one with Africa.

Today, the newest tent models have dispensed with awkward guy ropes and cumbersome support poles, thanks to an ingenious exterior frame. The threshold of even a modest tent today provides a shaded verandah for midday reading. The main compartment is generally laid out with two full-length spring-and-mattress beds, carpets on the floor, makeup tables. In the rear, a smaller room offers a private toilet (often a "long drop"), as well as the luxury of a custom-catered shower. And, yes, in all likelihood, the tent will be equipped with its own kindly retainer, bringing tea at dawn, fussing over your laundry, and making sure your shower is waiting for you after your last game drive of the day. And at night, when one seals the zippered front door, one has essentially created a *cordon sanitaire* against all predatory mammals, snakes, and insects.

I believe it is in every traveler's best interest to spend as many nights as possible under canvas. Be warned that many packaged tours avoid tented camps (a) because lodges are generally less expensive and (b) because most "first-timers," lacking guidance, might become hysterical if they were to find a mere swatch of canvas would be their only protection from the wild.

The cozy lodge of former years now caters to "one-night-stand" package tours.

I recently spent two nights at Ngulia Lodge in Tsavo West. Shortly after my arrival on the first night, fifty Italians piled out

of minibuses, looked at their watches, and proclaimed, "*Ora mangiare.*" The following evening their still-warm beds were claimed by fifty Germans whose main concern seemed to be the merits of White Cap beer. During dinner on these two consecutive nights, a leopard ghosted to the water hole in front of the lodge. Neither the Italians nor the Germans wished to be distracted from their meal by "a cat." Soon, the leopard, spooked by all the jabberwocky, vanished into the night.

As a postscript, Glen Cottar's historic tented camp exists to this day, albeit under different management. Now, while it is more luxurious than ever before—it even has a swimming pool—much has changed for the worst. In the morning following Alan Price's marathon joke session, we undertook a two-hour game drive during which we encountered twenty-six rhinos, three of which lowered their heads and charged the Land Rover. Everywhere there was a glut of elephants returning from the cambretum woodland to water in the Tsavo. Today, on my return, I was informed the last rhino sighted was five years previously; the last elephant, once the most common of all animals in Tsavo, three months previously. The present-day manager, sick with pneumonia, was dispirited, too. He repeated over and over, "Bloody poachers!" Today all that Glen Cottar's historic camp offers is bird-watching, good food, a dip in the pool, and ice-cold Tusker beer.

Luckily, there are many other tented camps in Africa that still have everything. Herewith a list of my favorites, broken down by country. Details of each are to be found in "Advisory: Hotels, Lodges, and Tented camps in Kenya, Tanzania, Zimbabwe, Zambia, and Botswana" (see p. 23). You should insist that your travel agent include more than one in your itinerary.

KENYA

MASAI MARA:
  LITTLE GOVERNOR'S CAMP
  KICHWA TEMBO
  FIG TREE CAMP
  GLEN COTTAR'S CAMP
  WILLIE ROBERTS' CAMP
LAKE BARINGO:
  ISLAND CAMP
SAMBURU:
  LARSEN'S CAMP
THE MATHEWS RANGE:
  KITICH
THE COAST:
  TANA DELTA CAMP
  KIWAYU

TANZANIA

TARANGIRE PARK:
  TARANGIRE CAMP
RUAHA:
  RUAHA CAMP

BOTSWANA

OKAVANGO DELTA:
  SHINDE ISLAND CAMP
  CAMP OKAVANGO
  MACHABA CAMP
  NXAMASERI
  CAMP MOREMI
  XUGANA CAMP

ZAMBIA

LUANGWA VALLEY NATIONAL PARK:
  TENA TENA CAMP

Cheetah near Kichwa Tembo, in Kenya's Masai Mara

A D V I S O R Y

Questions to Ask <u>Before</u> You Choose
a Group Safari

What is the limit on group size?

What types of people are likely to be on the trip?

What is/isn't included—all meals, accommodations?

Are there any hidden costs? (Park fees? liquor? fees for Masai Village?)

What types of vehicles are used for transportation and game drives?

Is everyone guaranteed at least one window seat and *access to the pop-up roof?*

How many people ride in each vehicle?

How much driving is there between lodges?

Is any walking/hiking allowed?

Will there be any night game drives?

How much free time will there be?

Are there any internal flights provided?

What is the refund policy for cancellations?

What plans are there for medical emergencies?

What percent of your business is customized safaris?

How would the price differ if I went on the same itinerary with a group of six friends?

Do you employ experienced naturalist-guides or just "driver-guides"?

How well do the guides speak English?

How long have you been operating tours to Kenya (or other destination)?

Do you operate your own tours or subcontract to a local operator?

How long have you been working with that local operator?

Is it possible to talk to clients from past trips?

How many people go on your safaris each year?

How far in advance do I have to reserve to get the cheapest fare?

What optional extensions are available, either through your group or another?

What will the weather be like?

What kinds of clothes/supplies/medicines do I need to bring?

Describe a typical day on your safari.

What would you say makes your company different from the rest?

A D V I S O R Y

Questions to Ask About Permanent Tented Camps and/or Tented Safaris

Do you use established campgrounds or set up your own camps in the wild? (Avoid operators who stick to campgrounds.)

Does each tent have its own shower and toilet facilities, or are they shared?

Are the toilets flush or "long drops"?

How far apart are the tents placed?

Are there cots/beds with sheets in the tents or just foam mats for sleeping bags?

Is there a place to hang up clothes?

How many beds does the camp have?

Does the staff do laundry?

Is there a generator, or is power provided by gas canisters and solar panels? (Noisy, unsound-proofed generators can spoil the peaceful wilderness atmosphere of a tented camp.)

Are the camp's accommodations native-style huts, cabins, or tents? (Airy huts built of native materials can be cooler and roomier than tents, which are really only necessary when you're moving from place to place. But some permanent tents, such as those at Governor's Camp in Kenya's Masai Mara, are very spacious and luxurious.)

A D V I S O R Y

Recommended Safari Operators

U.S. OPERATORS •

Abercrombie and Kent International, Inc.: *1420 Kensington Road, Oak Brook, IL 60521; tel. 312-954-2944 or 800-323-7308*

Africa Expeditions: *Frontiers, Box 161, Pearce Mill Road, Wexford, PA 15090; tel. 800-245-1950*

East Africa Safari Co.: *250 West 57th Street, New York, NY 10017; tel. 212-757-0722 or 800-772-3214*

Micato Safaris: *57 East 11th Street, New York, NY 10003; tel. 212-777-9292*

Overseas Adventure Travel: *349 Broadway, Cambridge, MA 02139; tel. 617-876-0533 or 800-221-0814*

Safari Camp Services, Ltd.: *Safari Center, 3201 North Sepulveda Boulevard, Manhattan Beach, CA 90266; tel. 213-546-4411*

Special Expeditions: *720 Fifth Avenue, Suite 605, New York, NY 10019; tel. 212-765-7740 or 800-762-0003*

A. K. Taylor International, Ltd.: *2724 Arvin Road, Billings, MT 59102; tel. 406-656-0706*

BOOKING AGENTS •

East Africa Safari Co.: *250 West 57th Street, New York, NY 10017; tel. 212-757-0722 or 800-772-3214*

Safari Consultants of London, Ltd.: *3535 Ridgelake Drive, Suite B, Metairie, LA 70002; tel. 800-648-6541*

Gametrackers International, Inc.: *1000 East Broadway, Glendale, CA 91205; tel. 213-622-8130 or 800-421-8907; telex 662769*

Into Africa, Inc: *93 Doubling Road, Greenwich, CT 06830; tel. 203-869-8165; Fax 203-625-9648*

OPERATORS
WITHIN AFRICA •

Bateleur Safaris: Box 42562, Nairobi, Kenya; tel. 254-2-27048. Personalized safaris.

David Peterson, Dorobo Tours and Safaris: Box 2534, Arusha, Tanzania; tel. 255-57-2300, telex 42018.

Flame Tree Safaris, Ltd.: Chrissie Aldrich, Box 82, Nanyuki, Kenya; tel. 254-176-22053. Personalized safaris.

Flamingo Tours of East Africa: 139A New Bond Street, London W1Y 9FB, England; tel. 44-1-409-2229. Group tours.

Inside Africa Safaris, Ltd.: Box 59767, Nairobi, Kenya; tel. 254-2-337154, telex 25788. Group tours and personalized safaris.

Ker and Downey Safaris: Box 41822, Nairobi, Kenya; tel. 254-2-340332 or 556466, telex 24223. Personalized safaris.

Danny McCallum, Olechugu Safaris Ltd.: P.O. Box 295, Nanyuki, Kenya; tel. Timau 24; telex 25583; Fax 245 176 23416 (night-time only).

Let's Go Travel: Box 60432, Nairobi, Kenya; tel. 254-2-29540, telex 25440. Rental cars.

Robin Hurt Safaris: Box 24988, Nairobi, Kenya; tel. 254-2-882826, telex 25583. Personalized safaris.

Sandy Cameron: Box 24874, Nairobi, Kenya; tel. 254-2-882625. Personalized safaris.

John Stevens: c/o Fothergill Island, Post Bag 2081, Kariba, Zimbabwe; telex 2253. Personalized wilderness trips.

Jed Robinson: P.O. Box 145, Victoria Falls, Zimbabwe; tel. 263-13-4486, telex 51667 SCSZW. Group wilderness trips.

Robin Pope Safaris, Ltd: P.O. Box 320154, Lusaka, Zambia. Personalized safaris and camp owner.

Tanzania Guides Ltd: Bjorn Figenshov, P.O. Box 2031, Arusha, Tanzania; tel. 255-57-69-62; FAX 255-57-75-04. Personalized safaris and group tours.

Tor Allan Safaris Ltd.: P.O. Box 41959, Nairobi, Kenya; tel. 254-2-891-190; telex COMPASS 22963. Personalized safaris.

Westminster Safaris: Via Lisa Cox, L. P. Gutteridge, Ltd., 34 Bermudiana Road, Hamilton, Bermuda HM11; tel. 809-295-4545, telex 290-3397.

Wildersun Safaris: *Box 930, Arusha, Tanzania; tel. 255-57-3880; telex 42126. Group tours.*
Willie Roberts: *Box 24513, Nairobi, Kenya; tel. 254-2-50613. Personalized safaris.*

A D V I S O R Y

Hotels, Lodges, and Tented Camps in Kenya, Tanzania, Zimbabwe, Zambia, and Botswana

The following hotels have been divided into four price categories to give a rough idea of costs. Rates may vary slightly, depending on how you book your trip—I recommend using one of the companies listed in the preceding advisory. Accommodations are categorized according to the price of a double room in high season (in U.S. dollars). Prices are per day, and generally include meals except in the city hotels.

Inexpensive ($) . . . . $30–$70
Moderate ($$) . . . . $70–$150
Expensive ($$$) . . . . $150–$300
Very expensive ($$$$) . . . . . $300 and up

K E N Y A •

Kenya, where the notion of the safari began, was home to the grandest one of all. In 1909, Teddy Roosevelt set out on a fifteen-month expedition that employed 500 porters and cost the equivalent of $1 million in today's money. Ever since then, Kenya has been the most popular safari country, and now draws nearly 700,000 visitors a year for many types of safaris, all admittedly on a somewhat less extravagant scale than

Roosevelt's. Despite the package-tour crowds, it's still possible to experience the country's amazingly varied terrain, culture, and wildlife in relative peace. The key is choosing the right operator and accommodations.

MASAI MARA

KICHWA TEMBO—THIS 42-TENT CAMP IS MOSTLY GEARED FOR PACKAGE TOURS AND, ALTHOUGH COMFORTABLE, LACKS SOME OF THE CHARM AND INTIMACY OF SMALLER CAMPS. THE BAR IS ALTERNATELY ALLURING AND OVERCROWDED, DEPENDING ON THE NUMBER AND SPIRITS OF CUSTOMERS. SEE "ROMANTIC HOTELS OF AFRICA," PAGE 109, FOR MORE INFORMATION. $$$ (P.O. BOX 59749, NAIROBI, KENYA; TEL. 254-2-334955)

LITTLE GOVERNOR'S CAMP—A LUXURIOUS, HIGHLY RECOMMENDED TENTED CAMP THAT IS SITUATED DOWN THE RIVER FROM THE MUCH LARGER GOVERNOR'S CAMP. IT'S SMALL AND ROMANTIC, WITH PERSONALIZED SERVICE. THREE OF THE 15 TENTS HERE EVEN HAVE DOUBLE BEDS, A RARITY IN AFRICA. $$$ (P.O. BOX 48217, NAIROBI; TEL. 254-2-331041)

GLEN COTTAR'S CAMP—NIGHT GAME DRIVES AND WALKS ARE THE SPECIALTY OF THIS 30-TENT CAMP, LOCATED JUST OUTSIDE THE RESERVE'S BOUNDARIES. $$$ (NAIROBI TRAVEL CENTER, P.O. BOX 41178, NAIROBI; TEL. 254-2-20255)

INTREPID'S CLUB—AN EXPENSIVE, SELECT CAMP WITH LARGE, COMFORTABLE TENTS AND GOOD FOOD, THIS "CLUB" NEVERTHELESS HAS A SLIGHTLY PHONY EDGE. $$$ (25 SYLVAN ROAD SOUTH, WESTPORT, CT 06880; TEL. 203-226-4186)

WILLIE ROBERTS' CAMP—PROBABLY THE MARA'S MOST EXPENSIVE CAMP AND MAY BE ITS BEST. RUN BY SAFARI OPERATOR AND WHEAT FARMER WILLIE ROB-

ERTS, THIS THATCHED-ROOFED, OPEN-AIR CAMP ON THE EDGE OF THE MARA OFFERS GREAT FOOD, SUPERB COMPANY, AND PRIVATE SAFARIS INTO THE RESERVE. ROBERTS ALSO OPERATES HALF-DAY FISHING TRIPS TO RUSINGA ISLAND ON LAKE VICTORIA, WHERE YOU CAN CATCH NILE PERCH. $$$$ (P.O. BOX 24513, NAIROBI, KENYA; TEL. 254-2-50613)

UP-COUNTRY

MT. KENYA SAFARI CLUB—THIS LUXURY COUNTRY "CLUB" OVERLOOKING MT. KENYA HAS METICULOUSLY LANDSCAPED GROUNDS, AN INVITING SWIMMING POOL, AND A FIREPLACE IN EVERY ROOM. IT ATTEMPTS TO RECREATE THE ATMOSPHERE OF THE COLONIAL DAYS BUT LACKS STYLE AND SUCCEEDS ONLY IN CREATING AN ARTIFICIAL AFRICA. OVERRATED. $$$ (NANYUKI, KENYA; TEL. 254-176-2141)

OL DONYO WUAS—RICK BONHAM'S EXOTIC NEW LODGE IN THE CHYULU HILLS. HIKE, RIDE, OR SEE GAME IN NEARBY TSAVO OR AMBOSELI, WHILE AVOIDING THE CROWDS IN THESE POPULAR PARKS. BONHAM ALSO GUIDES WALKING SAFARIS, A RARITY IN KENYA. $$$$ (P.O. BOX 24133, NAIROBI; TEL. 254-2-882521, OR BOOK VIA SAFARI CONSULTANTS OF LONDON, 3535 RIDGELAKE DRIVE, SUITE B, METAIRIE, LA 70002; TEL. 504-834-2444 OR 800-648-6541.)

LARSEN'S CAMP—YOU CAN ESCAPE THE HORDES AT THIS CAMP IN SAMBURU, WHERE YOU'LL SEE UNUSUAL DESERT SPECIES SUCH AS THE RETICULATED GIRAFFE AND GREVY'S ZEBRA. IT'S SMALL, SOPHISTICATED, AND EXPENSIVE, BUT SEEMS TO LACK A PERSONAL TOUCH AT TIMES. $$$ (BOOK THROUGH BLOCK HOTELS, P.O. BOX 47557, NAIROBI, KENYA; TEL. 254-2-331635)

ISLAND CAMP—A MODERATE YET CHARMING CAMP SET ON AN ISLAND IN THE MIDDLE OF LAKE BARINGO,

ISLAND CAMP OFFERS WATERSKIING, BOAT TRIPS, A HILL-TOP SWIMMING POOL WITH A BEAUTIFUL VIEW OF THE LAKE, INTERESTING FOOD, AND HOSPITABLE SERVICE. $$ (P.O. BOX 42475, NAIROBI, KENYA; TEL. 254-2-25641)

LION HILL CAMP—A TENTED CAMP AT LAKE NAKURU WITH ABOUT 60 BEDS AND A SWIMMING POOL. A DECENT PLACE TO STAY EN ROUTE TO SOMEWHERE ELSE. $$$ (P.O. BOX 7094, NAKURU, KENYA; CALL LET'S GO TRAVEL, TEL. 254-2-340331)

LEWA DOWNS—WITH JUST A FEW SIMPLE COTTAGES, THIS WORKING CATTLE RANCH NORTH OF NANYUKI AND SOUTH OF SAMBURU OFFERS EXTRAORDINARY HOSPITALITY, GOOD FOOD, A PRIVATE RHINO RESERVE, AND GAME-VIEWING BY HORSEBACK. $$$ (VIA BATELEUR SAFARIS, BOX 42562, NAIROBI, KENYA; TEL. 254-2-27048)

MERU MULIKA LODGE—AN INEXPENSIVE, BASIC LODGE THAT'S WORTH A STAY BECAUSE OF THE NATURAL BEAUTY OF RELATIVELY UNTRAVELED MERU NATIONAL PARK. GAME IS PLENTIFUL AND THE PARK IS HOME TO OVER 300 SPECIES OF BIRDS, MANY COLORFUL AND UNIQUE. YOU CAN OFTEN SEE ELEPHANTS, BUFFALO, ZEBRA AND BABOONS FROM THE TERRACE OF THE LODGE. VISITORS SHOULD EXERCISE EXTREME CAUTION, HOWEVER, BECAUSE AT PRESS TIME, POACHERS POSED A THREAT TO TRAVELERS IN SOME PARTS OF THE PARK. $ (BOOK VIA AFRICAN TOURS AND HOTELS, P.O. BOX 30471, NAIROBI; TEL. 254-2-742926)

LEOPARD ROCK LODGE—A "SELF-HELP CAMP," WHICH MEANS YOU MUST BRING YOUR OWN FOOD. COOKING UTENSILS ARE PROVIDED IN COTTAGE-STYLE HUTS SET UNDER ACACIA TREES. $ (A.A. TRAVEL LTD., P.O. BOX 14982, NAIROBI; TEL. 254-2-742926)

OASIS SAFARI CAMP—MEET EL MOLO, THE SMALLEST TRIBE IN KENYA, WHEN YOU STAY AT THIS BASIC LODGE IN THE HOT, DRY MOONSCAPE AROUND LAKE

TURKANA. FLYING IN IS THE BEST WAY TO GET THERE. $$ (C/O MUTHAIGA CONNECTION, P.O. BOX 34464, NAIROBI, KENYA; TEL. 254-2-750036)

KITICH CAMP—IN MATHEW'S RANGE TO THE NORTH, A THREE-HOUR DRIVE FROM SAMBURU, THIS BEAUTIFUL AND RELATIVELY INACCESSIBLE 10-TENT CAMP IS IN A PRIMARY FOREST WHERE YOU'RE LIKELY TO SEE LEOPARDS AT NIGHT. BUTTERFLIES AND ORCHIDS ABOUND, AND THE FOREST IS HOME TO A SMALL POPULATION OF ELEPHANTS AND RHINOS. SEE ANIMALS AS YOU WALK OVER FOREST PATHS AND SWIM IN A CLEAR, SPRING-FED NATURAL POOL—THE BEST SWIMMING HOLE IN KENYA. $$$ (VIA FLAME TREE SAFARIS, BOX 82, NANYUKI, KENYA; TEL. 254-176-22053)

SANGARE RANCH—FOR TOTAL PRIVACY AND LUXURY IN THE ABERDARES, HONEYMOONERS LIKE THIS TINY, 2-BEDROOM LODGE ON A RANCH OWNED BY MIKE AND JANE PRETTEJOHN. $$$ (P.O. BOX 24, MWEIGA, KENYA; TEL. 254-MWEIGA 20, OR BOOK IN THE U.S. THROUGH SAFARI CONSULTANTS; TEL. 504-834-2444 OR 800-648-6541)

THE ARK—THOUGH IT'S ON THE TOURIST CIRCUIT, THIS IS AN INTERESTING PLACE TO SPEND ONE NIGHT. THE PLEASANT DORMITORY-TYPE LODGE, BUILT IN THE SHAPE OF AN ARK, OVERLOOKS A FLOODLIT WATER HOLE WHERE YOU CAN WATCH ANIMALS COME TO DRINK AT NIGHT. THE FOOD IS DECENT, BUT THE BATHROOMS ARE SHARED. $$$ (SIGNET HOTELS, P.O. BOX 48690, NAIROBI; TEL. 254-2-335900)

ABERDARE COUNTRY CLUB—DESPITE THE FACT THAT TOURISTS SOMETIMES COME BY THE BUSLOAD, THIS "CLUB" RETAINS YESTERYEAR'S ATMOSPHERE AND CHARM. COMFORTABLE, SPACIOUS COTTAGES LOOK OUT ONTO PRETTY GROUNDS, AND A GOOD CURRY LUNCH IS SERVED ON SUNDAYS. SOME PEOPLE STOP IN JUST FOR LUNCH ON THE WAY TO THE ARK. $$$ (SIGNET HOTELS, P.O. BOX 48690, NAIROBI; TEL. 254-2-335900)

LOKITELA FARM—A TRADITIONAL FARMHOUSE ON MT. ELGON. RUN BY TONY MILLS, THIS BASIC BUT RELAXING AND FRIENDLY LODGE RECALLS THE OLD KENYA. WALKING TOURS, CAVES TO EXPLORE NEARBY. $$$ (BOX 122, KITALE, KENYA; CALL LET'S GO TRAVEL, TEL. 254-2-340331)

NAIROBI

FOR HOTELS IN CENTRAL NAIROBI, SEE "ADVISORY: WHERE TO DINE AND STAY IN NAIROBI" IN CHAPTER 10, "LEGEND OF NAIROBI" (PAGE 190).

NAIROBI OUTSKIRTS

KENTMERE CLUB—ALPINE FLOWERS FILL THE GARDENS AT THIS INEXPENSIVE, CHARMING TUDOR-STYLE HOTEL, WHICH STANDS ON THE ROLLING HILLS OF A TEA ESTATE AT 8000 FT. ELEVATION. 25 MINUTES BY CAR FROM NAIROBI. $ (P.O. BOX 39508, NAIROBI, KENYA; TEL. 254-2-42101)

FAIRVIEW HOTEL—ON THE OUTSKIRTS OF THE CITY, THIS INEXPENSIVE HOTEL HAS PRETTY GARDENS, A LIVELY BAR, AND OPPORTUNITIES FOR MEETING A CROSS-SECTION OF PEOPLE. $ (BOX 40842, NAIROBI; TEL. 254-2-723213)

GIRAFFE MANOR—HERE GIRAFFES NIBBLE THE LAWN OF AN ELEGANT, ENGLISH-STYLE COUNTRY HOUSE, PART OF A WILDLIFE CENTER RUN BY THE AFRICAN FUND FOR ENDANGERED WILDLIFE. VERY EXPENSIVE, BUT A GOOD CAUSE. $$$$ (P.O. BOX 15004, NAIROBI, KENYA; TEL. 254-2-891078, OR BOOK THROUGH AFEW, 1512 BOLTON STREET, BALTIMORE, MD 21217, TEL. 301-669-2276)

THE KENYA COAST

SEE "ADVISORY: UNUSUAL COASTAL HIDEAWAYS" IN
CHAPTER 11, "THE SECRET COAST" (PAGE 201).

T A N Z A N I A • Lodgings in Tanzania don't begin
to approach the standards of luxury and comfort one finds in Kenya.
With a very few exceptions, the best way to travel here is to spend as
much time as possible in the game-filled national parks (which make up
14 percent of the entire country) on a private tented safari with a
knowledgeable guide and outfitter.

DAR ES SALAAM

KILIMANJARO HOTEL—IF YOU CAN'T AVOID THE
CITY, STAY AT THE "KILI," BUT THE HOTELS ON THE COAST
ARE MUCH MORE PLEASANT, IF ONLY BECAUSE OF THEIR
SEASIDE SETTING. LOCK UP EVERYTHING YOU CAN; THIEV-
ERY IS COMMON IN THIS HOTEL. $$ (P.O. BOX 9312,
DAR ES SALAAM; TEL. 255-51-47101, TELEX 41185)

BAHARI BEACH HOTEL—A GOOD 45 MINUTES
NORTH OF DAR ES SALAAM, THIS ATTRACTIVE 100-BED-
ROOM HOTEL CONSISTS OF ROUND, TWO-STORY CHALETS
WITH THATCHED ROOFS, SET AMONG PALM TREES AND
OVERLOOKING THE INDIAN OCEAN. THE QUALITY OF THE
FOOD, SERVICE, AND AIR CONDITIONING VARIES FROM
DAY TO DAY. $$ (P.O. BOX 9313, DAR ES SALAAM; TEL.
255-51-47621)

KUNDUCHI BEACH HOTEL—A 100-ROOM GOV-
ERNMENT-RUN HOTEL OF ARABIC DESIGN, WITH MANY
TILE MURALS AND CARVED WOODEN DOORS. BEAUTIFUL
INDIAN OCEAN SETTING, BUT CRIME-RIDDEN. $$ (P.O.
BOX 9313, DAR ES SALAAM; TEL. 255-51-47621)

ARUSHA

THERE ARE SEVERAL HOTELS IN DOWNTOWN ARUSHA, BUT NONE WORTHY OF NOTE. YOUR BEST BET IS TO STAY AT ONE OF THE TWO GOOD LODGES THAT ARE ABOUT 15 MINUTES OUT OF TOWN.

MT. MERU GAME LODGE—THIS COZY AND ATTRACTIVE 23-BED LODGE IS WELL-RUN BY THE AMERICAN TOUR OPERATOR ABERCROMBIE AND KENT. IT'S A PLEASANT PLACE TO STAY AFTER A SAFARI OR A RUGGED CLIMB UP MT. KILIMANJARO. BUT TRY NOT TO BE THERE ON SATURDAY NIGHTS, WHEN AN ANNOYINGLY LOUD BAND PLAYS AT THE HOTEL NEXT DOOR. $$ (P.O. BOX 659, USA RIVER, TANZANIA; TEL. 255-963-43)

NGARE SERO MOUNTAIN LODGE—THE SNOWS OF KILIMANJARO PROVIDE THE BACKDROP FOR THIS FARMHOUSE DATING FROM THE GERMAN COLONIAL PERIOD AT THE TURN OF THE CENTURY. SET IN THE MIDST OF LUSH GARDENS AT AN ALTITUDE OF 4000 FEET ON MT. MERU, THE LODGE OFFERS DECENT FOOD, SLIGHTLY AUSTERE ACCOMMODATIONS, AND FASCINATING COMPANY. $$ (P.O. BOX 425, ARUSHA, TANZANIA; TEL. 255-USA RIVER 48)

NEAR MT. KILIMANJARO

KIBO HOTEL—VERY BASIC, BUT THE SHOWERS ARE HOT AND THE DINING ROOM MAKES A GOOD EFFORT. $$ (PRIVATE BAG, P.O. BOX 102, MOSHI, TANZANIA; TEL. 255-MARANGU 4)

MARANGU HOTEL—SMALL COTTAGES AND GREEN LAWNS; 2 MILES FROM KIBO HOTEL. $$ (P.O. BOX 40, MOSHI, TANZANIA; TEL. 255-MARANGU 11)

TARANGIRE NATIONAL PARK

TARANGIRE SAFARI LODGE—A PERMANENT TENTED CAMP THAT IS THE ONLY CATERING OFFERED IN THE PARK. NOW OWNED BY A LUTHERAN MISSIONARY AND A VOLVO DEALER FROM MINNEAPOLIS. AT TIMES IT IS VERY GOOD, AT OTHERS, FLYBLOWN. STUPENDOUS VIEWS OVERLOOKING THE RIVER VALLEY. YOU OFTEN SEE ELEPHANTS FROM THE VERANDAH. THE BEST TIME TO VISIT THIS PARK IS DURING THE DRY SEASON, FROM JUNE TO OCTOBER. $$ (BOX 1182, ARUSHA; TEL. 255-57-3090 OR -3625, TELEX 42038)

RUAHA NATIONAL PARK

RUAHA RIVER CAMP—A VERY RUSTIC, REMOTE CAMP OF CHARACTER, WHERE YOU'LL SEE PLENTY OF ANIMALS AND NO PEOPLE. $$ (% FOXTREKS, P.O. BOX 84, MUFINDI, TANZANIA; NO PHONE)

LAKE MANYARA NATIONAL PARK

LAKE MANYARA HOTEL—A LARGE HOTEL ON A CLIFF AT THE EDGE OF THE GREAT RIFT VALLEY WALL. THE PARK HAS FALLEN ON HARD TIMES DUE TO THE HEAVY POACHING OF ITS ELEPHANT POPULATION. BUT IT'S WORTH SPENDING A DAY THERE; YOU MAY SEE LIONS RESTING IN THE TREES. $$ (P.O. BOX 3100, ARUSHA; TEL. 255-57-501)

NGORONGORO CRATER

NGORONGORO CRATER LODGE—RECENTLY RENOVATED BY ABERCROMBIE AND KENT, THIS LODGE

PERCHES ON THE RIM OF THE CRATER, AT 7600 FEET ABOVE SEA LEVEL. ALL ROOMS LOOK OUT OVER THE VAST CRATER. BE PREPARED FOR CHILLY NIGHTS. $$ (P.O. BOX 427, ARUSHA, TANZANIA; TEL. 255-57-7803, EXT. 1234)

GIBB'S FARM—ONE OF EAST AFRICA'S ONLY AUTHENTIC COUNTRY INNS, WITH SOME CHARACTERS WHO SEEM TO HAVE LEAPED FROM THE PAGES OF E. M. FORSTER. IN CONTRAST TO MOST TANZANIAN LODGINGS, THIS ONE CONSISTENTLY MAINTAINS UNUSUALLY HIGH STANDARDS. MOST VISITORS STOP MERELY FOR THE EXTRAVAGANT LUNCHES OF COLD CURRIES, ASPARAGUS QUICHE, AND RHUBARB PIE. WHILE THERE IS LITTLE GAME TO BE SEEN IN THE GARDENS, A NIGHT AT THIS GLORIOUS OASIS WILL GIVE YOU A PEACEFUL RESPITE OF CRACKLING FIRES, TANTALIZING STORIES, AND THE SOUND OF BIRDSONG IN A FLAMBOYANT GARDEN OVERLOOKING A COFFEE ESTATE. JUST 15 MILES FROM NGORONGORO CRATER, THIS IS PRINCESS ANNE'S FAVORITE AFRICAN HOTEL. SEE "ADVISORY: A SPECIAL CASE OF ROMANCE," PAGE 114 $$ (P.O. BOX 1501, KARATU, TANZANIA; TEL. 255-KARATU 25, TELEX 42041)

SERENGETI PLAINS

NDUTU SAFARI LODGE—A LITTLE ROUGH, BUT A SMALL AND PLEASANT BASE CAMP ON THE EDGE OF THE SERENGETI, NEAR LAKE NDUTU. IT HAS PRETTY LAWNS, A COMFORTABLE OPEN-AIR BAR, PET GENET CATS THAT ROAM AROUND, AND ROOMS WITH BATHS. MY FAVORITE IN THE SERENGETI. $$ (P.O. BOX 1501, KARATU, TANZANIA; TEL 255-KARATU 25, TELEX 42041)

LOBO WILDLIFE LODGE—A HIGHLY UNUSUAL, DRAMATIC STRUCTURE BUILT RIGHT INTO A MASSIVE ROCK PROMONTORY ON A HILL ABOVE THE SERENGETI PLAIN. EVEN THE SWIMMING POOL IS CARVED OUT OF THE ROCK.

THE ROCK'S NATURAL CONTOURS FORM THE WALLS OF THE DINING ROOM AND BAR; WALKWAYS CONNECTING VARIOUS PARTS OF THE HOTEL TUNNEL THROUGH THE ROCK. $$ (BOX 3100, ARUSHA, TANZANIA, TEL. 255-57-3300)

GRUMETI RIVER CAMP—THIS 12-BED TENTED CAMP OVERLOOKING A HIPPO POOL IN THE REMOTE WESTERN SECTION OF THE PARK OFFERS AN UNUSUAL PERSPECTIVE ON A LESS CROWDED SECTION OF THE SERENGETI. THE FOOD IS GOOD, AND THOUGH THE CAMP LACKS SOME COMFORTS, IT HAS A CERTAIN CHARM. $$$ (P.O. BOX 48287, NAIROBI, KENYA; TEL. 254-2-891381)

ZANZIBAR

MNEMBA CLUB—DUE TO OPEN IN 1990. STAYING HERE WILL BE AKIN TO OWNING YOUR OWN ISLAND. TO GET THERE, YOU FIRST FLY TO ZANZIBAR, DRIVE 50 KILOMETERS, THEN TAKE A 10-MINUTE SAIL. $$$$ (P.O. BOX 48287, NAIROBI, KENYA; TEL. 254-2-891381)

OBEROI YA BWAWANI HOTEL—BARELY ADEQUATE HOTEL ON A ROCKY BEACH, WITHIN WALKING DISTANCE OF THE OLD STONE TOWN. SALTWATER POOL. $$ (P.O. BOX 670, ZANZIBAR, TEL. 255-54-30209)

ZAMBIA •

LUANGWA VALLEY NATIONAL PARK

DIVIDED INTO A NORTH AND SOUTH SECTION, THIS PARK IN NORTHEASTERN ZAMBIA OFFERS ONE OF THE LARGEST CONCENTRATIONS OF BOTH ELEPHANT AND BLACK RHINO

TO BE FOUND IN AFRICA TODAY. THE PARK IS KNOWN FOR ITS WELL-ORGANIZED FOOT SAFARIS AND NIGHT GAME DRIVES. UNTIL RECENTLY, LUANGWA HELD THE WORLD RECORD FOR THE GREATEST NUMBER OF SPECIES SPOTTED IN A 24-HOUR PERIOD. IN THE LIST BELOW, STARRED CAMPS ARE ESPECIALLY RECOMMENDED.

TENA TENA—THIS OFF-THE-BEATEN-TRACK TENTED CAMP WITH 12 BEDS OFFERS GOOD FOOD AND IS RUN BY TWO INTERESTING NATURALISTS, ROBIN POPE AND DAVID FOOT, WHO NOW SPEND PART OF THE YEAR OPERATING EXCELLENT SAFARIS IN MALAWI. MY FAVORITE IN THE LUANGWA. $$$ (P.O. BOX 320154, WOODLANDS, LUSAKA, ZAMBIA; NO PHONE)

MFUWE LODGE—ON A HIPPO- AND CROCODILE-FILLED LAGOON, AND MODERN **CHICHELE LODGE**, ON A HILL OVERLOOKING THE LUANGWA RIVER, HAVE ABOUT 60 BEDS EACH AND ARE MORE TOURISTY THAN THE MANY TENTED CAMPS AND SMALLER LODGES IN THIS AREA. $$ (BOOK LOCALLY THROUGH ZAMBIA NATIONAL TOURIST BOARD, CENTURY HOUSE, CAIRO ROAD, P.O. BOX 30017, LUSAKA, ZAMBIA; TEL. 260-1-217761)

CHIBEMBE LODGE—A MORE INTIMATE, 40-BED LODGE AND A BASE FOR WALKING SAFARIS RUN BY WILDERNESS TRAILS, WITH OVERNIGHTS IN TRAIL CAMPS. BUILT ON THE SCENIC BANKS OF THE LUANGWA RIVER ACROSS FROM THE PARK, CHIBEMBE HAS A POOL AND GROUNDS SHADED BY ENORMOUS EVERGREENS. $$ (BOOK THROUGH EAGLE TRAVEL, P.O. BOX 34530, LUSAKA, ZAMBIA; TEL. 260-1-214554; OR TWICKERS WORLD, 22 CHURCH STREET, TWICKENHAM, TW1 3NW, ENGLAND, TEL. 01-892-8164; OR ONE OF U.S. OPERATORS ON PAGE 21)

LUAMFWA LODGE—A 20-BED LODGE LOCATED IN VERY PRETTY COUNTRY IN THE SOUTH PART OF THE PARK. $$ (BOOK THROUGH ZAMBIA NATIONAL TOURIST BOARD, CENTURY HOUSE, CAIRO ROAD, P.O. BOX 30017, LUSAKA, ZAMBIA; TEL. 260-1-217761)

CHINZOMBO SAFARI CAMP—SLEEP IN ADOBE BUNGALOWS AT THIS FRIENDLY 22-BED CAMP OWNED BY SAVE THE RHINO TRUST. THE CAMP IS SITUATED JUST OUTSIDE THE PARK UNDER TALL SHADE TREES ON THE BANKS OF THE LUANGWA RIVER. PROFITS GO TO CONSERVATION EFFORTS. $$ (BOOK THROUGH T G TRAVEL, LTD., P.O. BOX 20104, KITWE, ZAMBIA; TEL. 260-1-212314 OR -215188, TELEX ZA51390)

KAPANI SAFARI CAMP—THE LEGENDARY AUTHOR/CONSERVATIONIST NORMAN CARR OWNS THIS LUXURIOUS RED-BRICK LODGE COMPLETE WITH SWIMMING POOL. THE SPACIOUS BEDROOMS HAVE FANS, TILE BATHS WITH SHOWERS, AND VERANDAHS. OFFERS DAY AND NIGHT GAME DRIVES, A NIGHT IN A NEARBY BUSH CAMP, WALKS, VISITS TO A NEARBY VILLAGE, NATURE TALKS. BUT IT'S ALMOST TOO LUXURIOUS FOR LUANGWA; GUESTS HERE LOSE SOME OF THE SENSATION OF THE WILD. $$ (BOOK LOCALLY THROUGH NORMAN CARR'S SAFARIS, P.O. BOX 100, MFUWE, ZAMBIA, OR CALL EAGLE TRAVEL IN LUSAKA, TEL. 260-1-214554)

NSEFU—SIX THATCHED RONDAVELS INSIDE THE SOUTHERN SECTION OF THE PARK, WHERE GAME ABOUNDS. $$ (BOOK THROUGH TWICKERS WORLD, 22 CHURCH STREET, TWICKENHAM, TW1 3NW, ENGLAND; TEL. 01-892-8164 OR ONE OF THE U.S. OPERATORS LISTED ON PAGE 21)

KAKULI—THERE ARE JUST 10 BEDS IN HUTS WITH THATCHED ROOFS AND PRIMITIVE PLUMBING IN THIS CAMP ON THE EDGE OF THE PARK. $$ (BOOK LOCALLY THROUGH EAGLE TRAVEL, P.O. BOX 34530, LUSAKA, ZAMBIA; TEL. 260-1-214554)

LUSAKA

SPEND AS LITTLE TIME AS POSSIBLE IN THIS CITY. IF YOU HAVE TO SPEND THE NIGHT, STAY AT THE **HOTEL**

INTERCONTINENTAL $$ (P.O. BOX 32201, LUSAKA, ZAMBIA; TEL. 260-1-212366) OR THE **PAMODZI** $$ (P.O. BOX 35450, LUSAKA, ZAMBIA; TEL. 260-1-21-26-20).

Z I M B A B W E ·

VICTORIA FALLS

VICTORIA FALLS HOTEL—A SOMEWHAT GARISH, 138-ROOM HOTEL THAT'S ALWAYS WORTH A STAY FOR ITS OLD WORLD STYLE AND PATHS LEADING TO SPECTACULAR VIEWS OF THE FALLS. $$. SEE "ROMANTIC HOTELS OF AFRICA," PAGE 103, FOR MORE INFORMATION. (P.O. BOX 10, VICTORIA FALLS, ZIMBABWE; TEL. 263-13-203 OR -204 OR -205; TELEX 3324)

IMBABALA CAMP—ABOUT AN HOUR UPSTREAM FROM THE FALLS, THIS SMALL, 14- TO 16-BED CAMP OF A-FRAMES IS RECOMMENDED FOR COUPLES. EACH HUT OVERLOOKS THE ZAMBEZI RIVER. THE CAMP HAS A POOL, AND OFFERS FISHING, GAME VIEWING BY BOAT, AND WALKING SAFARIS. $$ (BOOK LOCALLY THROUGH ZAMBEZI SAFARIS, P.O. BOX 159, VICTORIA FALLS, ZIMBABWE, TEL. 263-13-219)

MANA POOLS NATIONAL PARK

THIS GAME-FILLED PARK IN THE HEART OF THE ZAMBEZI VALLEY IS ALMOST AS UNSPOILED AS IT WAS WHEN I SAW IT FIRST 29 YEARS AGO. BECAUSE THE MANY ELEPHANTS WHO HAVE FOUND SANCTUARY THERE HAVE DENUDED EVERYTHING WITHIN THEIR REACH, YOU WON'T SEE MUCH SECONDARY GROWTH. YOU WILL SEE HIPPOS, RHINO, ANTELOPE, BUFFALO, LIONS, LEOPARDS, CHEETAH, AND WILD DOGS.

CHIKWENYA CAMP—AFRICA AS IT SHOULD BE. WITH JUST 16 BEDS, THIS CAMP'S SETTING IS SO OVER-RUN BY WILDLIFE THAT AN ARMED GUARD MUST ESCORT YOU FROM YOUR TENT TO THE MAIN LODGE. ELEPHANTS OR LIONS ARE LIKELY TO WANDER THROUGH CAMP; YOU'RE REALLY IN THE WILDERNESS HERE. LOCATED ON THE CONFLUENCE OF THE SAPI AND ZAMBEZI RIVERS ON THE EDGE OF THE PARK; EACH THATCHED HUT IN THE CAMP HAS A VIEW ACROSS THE WATER. $$ (BOOK THROUGH GAME TRAILS OF AFRICA, P.O. BOX 825, HARARE, ZIMBABWE; TEL. 263-4-705040)

B O T S W A N A ·

CHOBE NATIONAL PARK

CHOBE GAME LODGE—RICHARD BURTON AND ELIZABETH TAYLOR REMARRIED AT THIS ROMANTIC LODGE COMPLETE WITH AIR CONDITIONING, POOLS, AND GOOD FOOD. IT COMMANDS BEAUTIFUL VIEWS AND WILL SUIT THE LUXURY-MINDED. SEE "ROMANTIC HOTELS OF AFRICA," PAGE 112, FOR MORE INFORMATION. $$$ (P.O. BOX 782597, SANDTON 2146, SOUTH AFRICA; TEL. 27-331-3934/5; TELEX 8-6129SA)

CHOBE CHILWERO—LESS LUXURIOUS THAN THE CHOBE GAME LODGE, BUT THE COZY THATCHED HUTS HERE STILL OFFER ALL THE CREATURE COMFORTS. PERCHED ON THE GREEN ROLLING LAWNS OF A PROMONTORY, CHOBE CHILWERO OFFERS STRIKING VIEWS OF THE CHOBE RIVER FLOOD PLAIN AND OPPORTUNITIES FOR GREAT CLOSE-UP GAME-VIEWING. $$ (C/O CHOBE NATIONAL PARK, P.O. BOX 32, KASANE, BOTSWANA; TEL. 267-25-0340)

OKAVANGO DELTA

THIS EXTRAORDINARY NATURAL SURPRISE IS THE WORLD'S ONLY INLAND DELTA, FANNING OUT OVER NEARLY 7000 SQUARE MILES. AFTER SEARCHING IN VAIN FOR THE SEA, THE GIANT NETWORK OF MEANDERING STREAMS EVENTUALLY DISAPPEARS INTO A THICK CUSHION OF WHITE SAND. VISITORS RIDE OVER THE COOL, LUMINESCENT WATER BY DUGOUT CANOE OR OUTBOARD AND SEE GAME ON FOOT OR FROM A VEHICLE. THOUGH YOU CAN HEAR LIONS ROAR AT NIGHT AND SPOT OCCASIONAL ELEPHANT, BUFFALO, AND GIRAFFE, GAME IS NOT QUITE AS PROLIFIC HERE AS IN EAST AFRICA, BUT THE BIRDLIFE IS ASTOUNDING. THE OKAVANGO'S BEST ACCOMMODATIONS ARE SMALL TENTED CAMPS WITH 8 TO 14 BEDS, ACCESSIBLE MOSTLY BY CHARTERED PLANE. PLAN TO SPEND 5 TO 7 DAYS SEEING THE DELTA, AND SPLIT YOUR TIME BETWEEN JUST TWO CAMPS CHOSEN FROM THE MORE THAN 20 IN THE DELTA.

SHINDE CAMP—MY FAVORITE IN THE DELTA, THIS LUXURIOUS TENTED CAMP ON TRANQUIL, PALM-FRINGED SHINDE ISLAND OFFERS DELICIOUS BUSH CUISINE. BIRDLIFE AND BIG GAME ABOUND IN THIS REMOTE SETTING, UNDISTURBED BY TOURISM. $$ (BOOK THROUGH KER DOWNEY SELBY, 7701 WILTSHIRE PLACE DRIVE, SUITE 504, HOUSTON, TX 77040; TEL. 800-231-6352 OR 713-744-3527)

CAMP MOREMI—THIS LODGE, INCLUDING A "TREEHOUSE" WITH A COOL VERANDAH, IS HAND-CRAFTED FROM INDIGENOUS HARDWOODS AND KNOWN FOR ITS ATTENTION TO DETAIL. IT OVERLOOKS A LAGOON POPULATED BY EXTRAORDINARY WATERBIRDS. GAME DRIVES BY LAND ROVER TAKE YOU OVER ROADS OF THICK SAND PAST HERDS OF ELEPHANT AND BUFFALO. $$$ (DESERT AND DELTA SAFARIS, PRIVATE BAG 10, MAUN, BOTSWANA; TEL. 267-260-569 OR -564)

CAMP OKAVANGO—A PRETENTIOUS "5-STAR HOTEL UNDER CANVAS." WHILE COMFORTABLE AND LUX-

URIOUS, THIS "CAMP" TENDS TO MAKE YOU FEEL ISO-LATED FROM RATHER THAN IN TOUCH WITH THE AFRICAN WILDERNESS. $$$ (DESERT AND DELTA SAFARIS, 16179 EAST WHITTIER BOULEVARD, WHITTIER, CA 90603; TEL. 213-947-5100 OR PRIVATE BAG 10, MAUN, BOTSWANA; TEL. 267-260-569 OR -564)

XUGANA CAMP—A TENTED LODGE ON EDGE OF A PERMANENT SWAMP; HAS A HOUSEBOAT FOR RIVER TRIPS. $$ (O KAVANGO EXPLORATIONS, PRIVATE BAG 48, MAUN, BOTSWANA; TEL. 267-260-222 OR -205)

XAXABA—ANOTHER FAVORITE, THIS PLEASANT 9-HUT CAMP IN ONE OF WILDEST PARTS OF THE DELTA ON THE WESTERN EDGE OF CHIEF'S ISLAND. STARTING POINT FOR TRIPS UP AND DOWN THE BORO RIVER. $$ SEE "RO-MANTIC HOTELS OF AFRICA," PAGE 107 (P.O. BOX 147, MAUN, BOTSWANA; NO PHONE, TELEX 2482)

NXAMASERI—THERE ARE JUST 8 BEDS IN THIS THATCHED BUNGALOW CAMP KNOWN FOR ITS GOOD FISH-ING AND BIRD-WATCHING. OFFERS NIGHT-TIME BOAT RIDES AND A MENU THAT INCLUDES LOTS OF FRESH FISH. $$ (NXAMASERI, LTD., PRIVATE BAG 23, MAUN, BOTSWANA; TEL. 267-260-493)

MACHABA CAMP—JUST 12 GUESTS AT A TIME CAN STAY IN THIS LUXURIOUS TENTED CAMP ON THE BANKS OF THE KHWAI RIVER. WATCH A PROFUSION OF GAME COME TO DRINK FROM THE RIVER AT SUNSET. $$ (BOOK THROUGH KER DOWNEY SELBY, 7701 WILTSHIRE PLACE DRIVE, SUITE 504, HOUSTON, TX 77040; TEL. 800-231-6352 OR 713-744-3527)

Reference Map For Hotels, Lodges, and Tented Camps

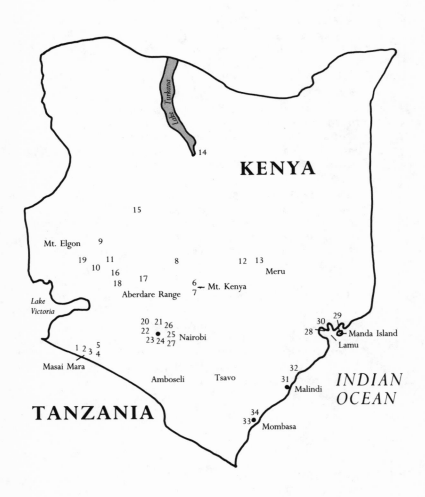

KENYA

14

15

Mt. Elgon   9

19   11
  10
    16   17
  18   6
Aberdare Range   7 — Mt. Kenya

8   12   13
                    Meru

Lake
Victoria

20   21
            26
22   25
23 24 27   Nairobi

30   29
28   Manda Island
        Lamu

1 2   5
      3   4

Masai Mara

Amboseli   Tsavo

32
31
    Malindi

INDIAN
OCEAN

TANZANIA

34
33   Mombasa

MAP LEGEND

KENYA

MASAI MARA
1 Kichwa Tembo
2 Little Governor's Camp
3 Glen Cottar's Camp
4 Intrepid's Club
5 Willie Roberts' Camp

CENTRAL KENYA
6 Mt. Kenya Safari Club
7 Ol Donyo Wuas
8 Larson's Camp
9 Island Camp
10 Lion Hill Camp
11 Lewa Downs
12 Meru Mulika Lodge
13 Leopard Rock Lodge
14 Oasis Safari Camp
15 Kitich Camp
16 Sangare Ranch
17 The Ark
18 Aberdare Country Club
19 Lokitela Farm

NAIROBI
20 Kentmere Club
21 Fairview Hotel
22 Giraffe Manor
23 The Norfolk
24 The Nairobi Safari Club
25 The Hilton
26 The Intercontinental
27 The Boulevard Hotel

THE COAST
28 Peponi Hotel: Lamu
29 Blue Safari Club: Manda
   Island
30 Kiwayu Mlango wa
   Chanu: Kiwayu Bay
31 Indian Ocean Lodge:
   Malindi
32 Tana Delta Camp

MOMBASA
33 Castle Hotel
34 Nyali Beach Hotel

TANZANIA

DAR ES SALAAM
35 Kilimanjaro Hotel
36 Bahari Beach Hotel
37 Kunduchi Beach Hotel

ARUSHA
38 Mt. Meru Game Lodge
39 Ngare Sero Mountain
   Lodge

BASE OF KILIMANJARO
40 Kibo Hotel
41 Marangu Hotel

RUAHA NATIONAL PARK
42 Ruaha River Camp

TARANGIRE NATIONAL
PARK
43 Tarangire Safari Lodge

LAKE MANYARA
NATIONAL PARK
44 Lake Manyara Hotel

NGORONGORO CRATER
45 Ngorongoro Crater Lodge
46 Gibb's Farm

Lake
Victoria

47   Serengeti
49 48

40 41   Mt. Kilimanjaro
Ngorongoro Crater — 45   39 38 — Arusha
46
43   51
Lake Manyara   44   50 ◯ **ZANZIBAR**

Lake
Tangan ka   36
TANZANIA   37
35 ● Dar es Salaam

*INDIAN
OCEAN*

42
Ruaha National
Park

60 54 52
58 59 57
53 55   — Luangwa Valley
56

ZAMBIA

61 ● Lusaka
62
65

Chobe
National Park   Victoria Falls   Harare ●
Okavanga   71 68   66 67   63 64
Delta   69 72   **ZIMBABWE**
70 74 ● Maun
73   Bulawayo ●

BOTSWANA

Sᴍᴀʟʟ Lᴀᴍᴜ ᴅʜᴏᴡ, SAILING IN THE WATERS OFF THE COAST OF Kᴇɴʏᴀ

A D V I S O R Y

Painless Africa: Preparing for Safari

No matter how accepted a cowboy hat may be in Reno, it will not do for Africa. The same goes for many articles of clothing that, at first glance, would seem perfectly appropriate for the bush. Most travel agents will be little help in advising you about clothing and accoutrements. No doubt, when they made their one and only trip to Africa, they failed to notice the hysteria greeting them as they sauntered across the verandah of Nairobi's Norfolk Hotel in pith helmet and puttees. Even worse, they may well fail to remind you that Africa breaks the rules of weather.

The big issue is not so much to look the part but to be comfortable at all times. And there is more to comfort than just clothing.

Here are some of the considerations you should make as you pack for safari:

- Africa can be hot.
- In the evening Africa can be cold.
- White clothing shows the dust.
- Black clothing absorbs the heat.
- The fierce midday sun is worthy of no less than a number 15 sunblock.
- In spite of everyone's promises about dependable weather systems, you may encounter rain.
- You will probably be traveling shoulder-to-shoulder with fellow travelers in vehicles and light planes.
- There will be a 30- to 40-pound baggage weight limit in small aircraft.
- The baggage containers on light aircraft prefer "squashable" luggage.
- You will encounter semiformal occasions at certain lodges and in cities.
- Occasionally, there will be flies in daylight, mosquitoes after dark.

- Prescription drugs can rarely be obtained in Africa.
- You should begin your malaria prophylactic regime *two weeks before* leaving, and you should allow yourself a spare supply on safari.
- Bottled water may not be available in Tanzania and Zambia.
- Food in Africa is remarkably palatable, and it is doubtful that you will lose weight on safari.
- You will probably lose your one and only hat.

In your luggage you should include:

- Sleeping pills if night noises keep you awake.
- Diarrhea medicine (such as Lomotil)—not because diarrhea is in your future, but because the medicine's accessibility will reassure you.
- Other medicines for the skittish: Band-aids, antibacterial ointment, hydrogen peroxide, alcohol swabs, antibiotics, aspirin, cortisone cream for bug bites, and water-purification tablets if you plan rough camping. (Incidentally, water purification pills don't always work: Use them only if there is nothing but foul water to drink.)
- Sunscreen with high SPF for body and lips.
- Paperback reading materials if afternoon siestas are not for you.
- Twice as much film as you expect to use.
- A telephoto lens not less than 300 mm. if you are seeking to film full-frame shots of wildlife.
- A spare lens cap.
- A small dependable flashlight with an extra set of long-life batteries.
- A pair of field glasses—not less than $6 \times$, preferably $8 \times$.
- A traveling combination lock for your suitcase containing money and passport.
- One down vest and one hardy sweater.
- Sports shirts with few synthetic components.
- At least three pairs of shorts.
- One pair of shoes comfortable enough for extended walking.
- Another light pair—possibly sandals—for knocking about in camp.
- Two crushable hats (usually available in Africa).
- A bandana.

- Packets of laundry soap.
- Muskoil insect repellent, or any brand containing 100 percent DEET (which, sadly, can cause a skin rash for some).
- A quick-drying bathing suit.
- A large bag of hard candy to give away to children en route, plus nonperishable, noncrushable snacks such as peanut M&M's or granola bars to be saved as energy-boosters when hiking or waiting at a border post for some unaccountable delay.
- A collection of T-shirts or inexpensive electronic devices, such as watches, to be donated to camp staff for heroic service.
- A large supply ($25 to $50) of $1 bills in American currency for occasional gratuities, and at least two $10 bills for crossing borders and for airport tax when leaving.

Bear in mind:

- You should avoid wearing whites, yellows, reds, and other brilliant colors on safari as they may alarm wildlife.
- Women's dresses and skirts are best drip-dry.
- In daylight hours shorts are far more comfortable and appropriate in Africa than long trousers.
- The African staff in tented camps will wash all your laundry with the exception of women's underwear.
- Camouflage clothing, which often is standard wear for revolutionaries, is not acceptable wear in many African countries.
- In most lodges, valuables can be left in the manager's safe.
- Color film is about four times more expensive when purchased in Africa than at home.
- You should be prepared to tip camp staff and your guide at the end of the safari.
- You should ask your Kenya tour operator whether or not he is in possession of a blanket Flying Doctors Service insurance policy. If not, sign up individually while in Nairobi for this very reasonable guarantee of an emergency airlift in the unlikely event of an accident.
- If your safari is confined mostly to vehicles, plan an exercise program that can be performed in the confines of your tent or on its verandah

during the afternoon. Alternatively, you may be allowed to jog ahead of the safari vehicle a few minutes each day. Cardiovascular exercise of any kind is a suitable balance to the good food and sedentary routine of game-watching.

- Kenyan, Tanzanian, Zambian, Zimbabwean, and Botswana currency are of no value except in the country of origin. Keep your local currency "float" to a minimum.

Most safaris begin in cities. In some, last-minute articles of clothing can be purchased:

- Nairobi and Harare are ideal starting points, since almost all your needs can be met in their stores.
- In Arusha, Victoria Falls, and Maun, stores offer a very limited variety of safari essentials.
- In Dar es Salaam and Lusaka, there are virtually no safari essentials to be found.

Specifically:

- In Nairobi, I recommend a visit to **Esquire Ltd**. (P.O. Box 41247, Nairobi, tel. 254-2-25727) for shorts, squashable bush hats, and bush jackets—a great luxury on safari. Mickie Migdoll, the manager, should be able to arrange the custom tailoring of a bush jacket within twenty-four hours, at a very reasonable price. **Ahamed Brothers** is another good outlet for ready-to-wear bush wear.

If you really want to look the part and be comfortable at the same time, pay a visit to an innocuous-looking shoe shop called **Pitamber Khoda** on Nairobi's Tom Mboya Street. Mr. Khoda's children still make *chopplis*, the leather sandal popularized by Gurkha foot soldiers in Afghanistan and brought to Kenya in 1925 by a British colonel. Today, *chopplis* are the preferred bush shoe of safari guides and professional hunters. While they give you little protection from thorns, these leather sandals keep your feet cool and well supported in all African terrain. What's more, they make long walks a joy. A custom pair, complete in about four days, may cost you about $40. If you are pressed for time, Pitamber Khoda's son may show you his selection of ready-to-wear *chopplis*. I would be very sad if ever I heard that Pitamber Khoda had gone out of business: In my travels through Africa I have already worn out four pairs made by his splendid artisans. (If you don't have time to wait for shoes to be made in Nairobi, as an alternative, I recommend any hiking shoes, especially "Topsiders," made by Rockport of Maine.)

While you are poking through the hurly-burly of Tom Mboya Street, I would suggest you drop by any of the textile shops to ask for a *kanga, kitenge*, or a *kikoi*. Each is a brightly colored fabric that, on women, can be worn as either a wrap, a dress, or a skirt, on men, as a kind of sarong. I wear *kikois* instead of pyjamas. On safari they are perfect evening wear to keep mosquitoes off one's legs, to avoid bare legs being fried by the campfire, and for the satisfaction of knowing you are more comfortable than anyone else. I usually carry a black one to be worn with a blazer for formal occasions on safari and bold blue and green ones for other evenings. For those men who regard the wearing of a "skirt" an affront to one's masculinity, buy one anyway: After a few days with friends in a tented camp, it is almost certain your attitude will change.

In Harare, within walking distance from Meikles' and the Monomatopa Hotels, are a number of clothing stores where all your outfitting needs can be filled. Zimbabweans are sticklers for khaki. For little money you should be able to buy shirt, shorts, long socks, and *veldtskoon* shoes (known elsewhere as desert boots), all in the same buff military color. Here it is also possible to purchase a classic pith helmet. Frankly, I find these archaic headpieces both cumbersome and unnecessary. Instead, buy two khaki bush hats (the second one in the event the first is lost) and you will be much better served.

• As a veteran of several bouts of malaria, I consider myself (in hindsight) reasonably well qualified to advise you how to avoid this unpleasant parasitic disease.

For everyday malaria, the only prophylactics available in the United States are *chloroquine* and *Aralen*, a prescription drug that needs to be taken once a week on the same day, starting two weeks before your trip and continuing for six weeks afterward. Take it but by no means consider yourself fully protected from malaria. I am told it has only 20 to 30 percent effectiveness.

In addition, while in London, Nairobi, or Harare, buy *Paludrine*, an over-the-counter drug that should be taken every day at sunset when on safari. Paludrine, I am told, has an 80 percent effectiveness rate.

In addition, your regular doctor will probably advise you to carry a short course of *Fansidar* (about three rather expensive and potent pills). These are targeted to the falsiparian form of the parasitic disease, a form that is quinine-resistant. In all likelihood, you will never have to take these pills since they are to be used only if you exhibit malarial symptoms—dizziness, aching joints, high fever, hot and cold spells, loss of appetite, and upset stomach. *Fansidar* is a precaution against an increasingly common form of the disease.

Check with the Centers for Disease Control (CDC) in Atlanta, Georgia, before you go, to see what strains of malaria are currently prevalent in the areas you are planning to visit, and what the latest developments in prophylactics are (404-639-2572). Or, call International Health Care, which is part of New York Hospital, at 212-746-1601, or the U.S. Public Health Service at 718-917-1685.

Almost all guides in Africa keep a first-aid kit and almost all safaris are without medical incident. Remind yourself from the beginning that the real adventure of this continent will, if you are prepared and relaxed, not be a health adventure.

A D V I S O R Y

Third World Food Precautions
for the Super-Jittery

Do not ever drink any unboiled water. (You'll be told it's okay to drink tap water in Nairobi, but why take a chance?)

This means do not have a drink with ice cubes in it.

Do not drink anything that may be mixed with tap water, such as lemonade, or any fruit juice that's not in a can.

Order soft drinks and beer in the bottle; then check and make sure your glass is completely dry before pouring it in.

Brush your teeth with bottled water or club soda or tea.

Do not open your mouth in the shower.

Make sure meat and vegetables are well cooked.

In East Africa, avoid fish dishes upcountry and meat dishes at the coast.

Avoid dairy products. (Many Third World countries don't pasteurize—but in Kenya, dairy products such as milk, cheese, and yogurt are safe.)

Do not eat fresh vegetables or fruits unless you peel them yourself. (This means no salads—lettuce may be washed in contaminated water.)

Frequent travelers to the Third World live by this rule: Cook it, boil it, peel it, or forget it! In Kenya, you may be able to break some of these rules and stay healthy. Sticking to these rules doesn't mean you don't have a chance of picking up some exotic disease, either. Use your own judgment, and before you go, discuss food precautions with your doctor, your safari company, and a number of people who have traveled there. I for one have never followed *any* of the above rules and am considered by my doctor to be very healthy, but you may not be so lucky.

W ILD DOGS IN THE SERENGETI

2

SERENGETI DID NOT DIE:

An Update on the Earth's Largest Terrestrial Migration

THERE WAS ONCE A TIME WHEN THE NAME "Serengeti" made hearts beat fast. Two men, Bernhard and Michael Grzimek, the former in his late forties, the latter his twenty-six-year-old son, coauthored a book and a film that rang with its poetry some thirty years ago. *Serengeti Shall Not Die* brought these vast plains of Tanzania to the attention of Europeans and Americans only just awakening to the realization that the animals of Africa were endangered less by the gun than by human encroachment. Michael—that reckless, laughing, dedicated conservationist— became, in the end, Serengeti's first martyr when his zebra-striped airplane collided with a griffon vulture and plummeted to earth. Quite possibly, his death ennobled the cause of conservation and turned this once little-known savannah into a legend, a paradox of animal behavior, habitat use, and human sacrifice.

But that was in 1959, and some memories are short. The wildebeest migration, which the boundaries of the Serengeti were intended to secure, varied its course. The country emerged from colonialism and, for nearly two decades, became the laboratory for a new economic order called African Socialism. Tanzania's frontier with its East African neighbor to the north, Kenya, closed and for over ten years, overseas tourists, one source of the national parks' staying power, avoided this penurious and slightly hostile nation. Today, *Serengeti Shall Not Die* is out of print, the access roads to the park are mined with potholes, game poaching on Serengeti's borders has increased dramatically, the lavish government hotels, built to accommodate herds of tourists, are usually unable to provide either running water or a square meal, and the memorial to Michael, proclaiming that "he gave all he possessed to the wild animals of Africa, including his life," is often obscured by high grass. Two years ago one reporter warned that the Serengeti National Park was "threatened with collapse."

But somehow—miraculously—delicate and interrelated forces that power this fragile ecosystem have not recognized human transgressions or warnings. Through sheer misadventure, it would seem, the wildebeest migration that stirred the Grzimeks in the late fifties, has grown at least six times during the intervening years. Today the flat expanse that separates one Serengeti horizon from another is no longer broad enough to contain this advancing army of ungulates. Only from an airplane with a full tank of petrol—precious stuff in today's Tanzania—can a human comprehend the extent of the migration, and even then the view is usually incomplete. Nature, it would seem, is not only profligate, but capricious; against heavy odds, the Serengeti has flatly refused to die, even though its wildebeest plunge headlong into a world that seems to have little room for large-scale terrestrial migrations.

I doubt whether even the most travel-weary visitor can fail to be stirred by this spectacle, the greatest assemblage of grazing animals on Earth. One February dawn, surrounded by a typical pod of about 10,000 wildebeest and zebra, I had the feeling I belonged to an era of our planet's history when man was merely one dot on a far horizon. Everywhere, as far as I could see, our species' much-bruited hegemony over all the world's creatures became a dubious memory. Here quadrupeds were clustered around me so thickly that watching them made me seasick. Most of the herd, feeding on old grass, was composed of females heavy with calves. Every afternoon for the last week I had seen them looking east, towards towering thunderheads looming over Ngorongoro. And in the evenings they followed the course of these clouds and their lightning bolts, into ionized air smelling of rain, hoping, it seemed, to find emerging new grass. These fruitless journeys after localized storms resembled huge zig-zags on the map of south-

eastern Serengeti and now, one week later, this herd was where it had begun and the rain was still to come.

The wildebeest calve each year in sequence with the first rains. In many years all the calves—sometimes nearly half a million—are born within a three-week period, and most of these during three halcyon days. This strategy allows the lactating females to exploit grass at the moment it attains its highest protein and calcium content.

This year the rains are late and so is the calving. As the wildebeest graze, their lowing sounds like a chorus of giant frogs. When they stop to size me up, they shake their long bladder-shaped faces over and over, as if trying to deny me something. Both males and females have straggly beards, and as they walk they hobble. Nothing fits. In Alan Root's classic wildlife film, *The Year of the Wildebeest*, he describes this seemingly comic creature as having "been put together out of spare parts by a committee." To add to this image of lovable buffoon, one yearling wildebeest gallops through the tightly packed grazers, bent, it would seem, on some madcap escapade. And while he runs, he bucks and swirls, spinning on his forefeet, as if a cinch has just been tightened around his hindquarters. Is he bothered by flies? Does he know of a secret danger? Or is he merely having fun? No one seems to care: Not one wildebeest looks up.

The other anomaly in the herd is a just-born calf, two minutes old. It is the herd's first and it inspires quite a different kind of behavior. As it tries to rise to its feet, eleven expectant mothers abandon their grazing to sniff. Clearly a curiosity, the wildebeest calf is several tones lighter in color than an adult. Two minutes after our finding it, it rises to its forefeet, which after a moment wobble and collapse; the calf is crushed into an awkward sitting position. At the age of five minutes, it tries again, and this time the youngster manages to splay its hindlegs, teetering for a moment longer. The next three minutes, once it has its first gulp of colostrum, are clearly the most important in its early development,

and by the time it is eight minutes old—almost to the second—
it has learned to run as fast as its mother.

Unlike the Burchell's zebra, scattered through the herd, wildebeest mothers generally reject their calf if it is unable to make
this quantum leap of motor development in the first ten minutes
of life. Shortly after we saw this youngster run helter-skelter beside
its mother, we came upon another not so successful. It was lying
in tall grass, and were it not for the driver's sharp eyes, we might
have run it over. Lying beside its afterbirth, it was still wet.
Lumpheaded, it looked at us, blinked its eyes and made no effort
to rise. We retreated out of sight to see which of the nearby
wildebeest mothers would claim it. One briefly moved in its direction
and raised our spirits. But she was searching only for some niblet
of grass, not for a calf. Clearly, this youngster had not risen to its
feet within the requisite ten minutes of life; such an early failure
is, no doubt, the symptomatic result of a developmental flaw. So it
is: Nature has made wildebeest mothers ruthless judges. All of a
sudden, a martial eagle spotted the calf and soon the sky filled
with vultures.

To watch the beginning of life on the Serengeti is to be acutely
aware of death. Lions, cheetahs, leopards, spotted hyenas, golden
jackals, Cape hunting dogs—they all seem to anticipate the birth
of so much tender protein. While most lions are territorial, there
are a few who have developed a strategy of following the wildebeest
herd and exploiting its profligacy with life. Generally they idle away
the sunlight hours, asleep in the shade, within earshot of the herd's
bleating. Their full stomachs and blood-stained whiskers would
suggest that at least every other night, on average, they cull one
more incautious wildebeest from the herd.

Predators are not the only cause of early death. In February
1973, some 3000 newborn calves drowned when their mothers
chose to swim them across Lake Lagarja. The lake is no major
obstacle; a detour of some three miles might have spared them
the tragedy. Nor is the lake particularly deep. But when the elder

wildebeest forded the alkaline waters, they did so en masse. Mothers soon became separated from their young, and these, arrived at the far bank, then turned around to swim back in search of their lost parent. The result was chaos, and a windfall for the resident leopards.

Such natural disasters have little effect on wildebeest numbers. Three thousand out of nearly a million and a half is statistically insignificant. And while the casual observer notes a colossal number of kills by predators in the Serengeti, these migrating wildebeest, it has been shown, are better off than more settled members of their species. In the 1970s, biologist Richard Bell concluded that the nonmigratory wildebeest of the Ngorongoro Crater lost 10 percent of their population annually to predators, while among the migrants of the Serengeti, a mere 1 percent perished. Moving, one supposes, is a strategy of survival.

But, clearly, moving has other rewards. One is struck—not so much in February, but later, during the dry season—how the wildebeest prefer running to walking. Dr. A.R.E. Sinclair, of the University of British Columbia, monitored the wildebeest during the 1970s. He believes that running is an adaptation to the Serengeti's grazing timetable and to the vast distances that separate one sequence of grassland from another. Only by moving at breakneck speed can the enormous herd cover the ground and thus exploit all available food resources. Indeed, if these wildebeest did not migrate, the Serengeti would be able to support only a fraction of what it can today. The behavior pattern of this wild herd resembles what today is being induced among cattle herds by America's most sophisticated cattlemen. Called "intensive rotational grazing," it artificially creates what the wildebeest migration has achieved naturally—a maximum stocking rate on a finite land resource.

For most who live throughout the year with the wildebeest, the experience of observing their epic march never pales. Dr. Markus Borner, who has resided at Seronera in the middle of the Serengeti for almost a decade, admits he is still overwhelmed by the wildebeest's success. "It looks like such a stupid animal," he says, sucking on a monstrous unlit pipe. "But as a herd it has developed unparalleled wisdom." Chief representative of Professor Bernhard Grzimek's Frankfurt Zoological Society, Dr. Borner is a slight man, given more to asking questions than handing down verdicts. The one gold earring and the disheveled hair seem to declare nothing more than the owner's aversion to pretense. He, his wife, young son and daughter occupy a cluttered bungalow whose lawn is often grazed by wildebeest. And when the herd is to the east on the open plains, much of Borner's day is spent overflying it in his Cessna—plotting its course and continuing the census work of Dr. Sinclair.

"It's really quite an elegant system the wildebeest have created," he says. "Now as they await the rains the herds congregate in splintered groups across the southeastern corner of the Serengeti and out into the Maswa Game Reserve. They'll stay there, for, of all types of country, they prefer the short- and medium-grass plains, where they can see for miles. When this country dries up, let's say in May, they move northwest—long threads of them—and then northeast through woodlands (which they don't particularly care for but which provides tall dry-season grass) across the border into Kenya. By August, there the Masai Mara is mobbed by them; a month or so later they start the return, back across the border, to reach the Serengeti's southeastern corner in times for the rains."

While the straight-line distance covered does not appear vast—perhaps 300 to 400 miles—Borner noted that the wildebeest move erratically and that the real distance covered might be closer to 1000 miles each year. "There're some old bulls out here who must be fifteen years old. Just imagine all the miles they've run!"

Borner pointed out that the Serengeti is, by itself, not that rich a grassland. The soil is essentially hardpan, being the depository for the last several million years of ash from a nearby volcano, called Lengai. Trees rarely survive—only shallow-rooted grasses. For much of the year, when the herds have departed, the Serengeti resembles a desert. "But don't be fooled," added Borner. "In most

years the wildebeest—even the colossal number we're seeing at present—do not overgraze. In fact, their grazing probably stimulates grass production."

But the wildebeest do not migrate alone. The 200,000 zebra that precede them in effect prepare the grazing for wildebeest palates. Because the zebra are not ruminants, they can digest high new grass—often of poor quality and liquefied—more successfully than the wildebeest. By removing the coarse tops, they permit the wildebeest, who follow, access to the more succulent and nutritious leaves in the medium-height grasses. In turn, the wildebeest leave behind very short grasses, the food of choice for nearly a half million gazelles bringing up the rear.

"We think the population is more or less healthy right now," admits Dr. Borner. "But we're not altogether sure. Possibly there's been a reduction in the number of gazelle, as a result of the increase in the wildebeest population. In addition, we suspect there's about to be a food shortage in the north [in Kenya's Masai Mara], but again we're moving in the dark."

Dr. Borner's present uncertainty is mostly a result of the Tanzanian economy. Once a large scientific team, the Serengeti Research Institute, was stationed here at Seronera, partly to monitor the dynamics of the migration. Budget cuts in the 1970s, as well as political interference, discouraged much of the expensive research, and today SRI has become a randomly administered facility, catering to a few scientists working on their own, unrelated research. However, this stalemate at SRI may soon change. The Frankfurt Zoological Society recently introduced new management-related research tailored to monitor changes in animal numbers, health, and behavior, in the hopes of staving off any potential "crash." "The new director of National Parks, David Babu, is giving us the kind of encouragement we haven't had in years," says Borner. "He knows, as we do, that right now there might be a dramatic die-off of the wildebeest and we wouldn't realize it until it was well under way."

After meeting with Borner, I spent a day with a pack of fifteen

Cape hunting dogs. Eight were adults, seven yearlings. All morning, they lay up in the crannies of a small kopje, rocky outcrops, or *inselbergs*, that every few miles pimple the flat surface of the Serengeti. Unlike most other predators, wild dogs generally live together in absolute harmony. The young usually greet their elders with ritual submissiveness, and acts of hostility or insubordination are rare. The rules of behavior seem to be laid out quietly, with subtle canine courtesy.

But when wild dogs kill, all gentility vanishes. For miles they lope at 10 kilometers an hour. And when they run in pursuit of a quarry, few motorized vehicles can keep up. Their victim, as I watched: a just-born Thomson gazelle. They harried it in a broad circle, with each dog spelling the other in relays. In two minutes the animal was beaten. No more than a minute and a half later, all that remained was one femur. Among the wild dogs there was no scrapping for leftovers. In fact, the female who possessed the femur was mounted by a young male. And for the rest of the afternoon, the dogs resumed a civil way of life, lying next to a pool of water, wagging ears and tails, and whining with excitement whenever one drew near another.

"The wild dog is the most endangered predator in the Serengeti," Borner had told me. In Kenya, many of the old-school British game wardens had shot them on sight because they disapproved of their technique of killing. For years the Serengeti maintained its population by dint of having a more enlightened warden, and then suddenly within the last decade, in postcolonial times, dog numbers have declined. In all the Serengeti's 5600 square miles there may be as few as eighty. Next door, in Kenya's Mara, there are none. "I think it may be distemper, but one can't be sure," explained Dr. Borner. "You see, that's the kind of uncertainty our new monitoring project can attempt to correct."

Markus Borner is the first to admit that the Serengeti's great success today owes much to chance. "It is pure luck, good fortune—call it what you will—that these plains have been protected and the wildebeest migration endures. If today we had to

establish the Serengeti National Park all over again, it would already be too late."

The marvel of Serengeti is its innocuous brushstroke of time-lessness. Here in a country whose population increases annually at over 3 percent, these plains seem to defy history. Yes, there may be a few roads, a scattering of buildings at Seronera and Banagi, a grass airstrip here and there, but in over 97 percent of the Serengeti, man's hand is invisible. While across the border in Kenya, tourist minibuses are connected like link sausages as they encircle drowsy lions, here tourists are scarce and lions sleep unseen. On the Serengeti one watches the evening storms brew in the highlands to the east; one listens to a dustdevil scurry past, like a departing spirit; one mistakes 100,000 wildebeest for the shadow of a cloud; and all the time one thinks, "This is how it has always been."

But not always. A horn core and part of a skull of *megalotragus*, a large version of today's wildebeest, was found in the Olduvai Gorge, on the edge of the Serengeti Plains. It was dated at 1.5 million years and, from associated strata, it leads us to believe that, like today's wildebeest, it was a creature of seasons. From the oral tradition of the Masai we can extrapolate that during the nineteenth century the migration was very extensive—perhaps stretching far-ther north than it does today. But in 1890 there began what Dr. A.R.E. Sinclair describes as "a series of events of such profound ecological importance that the repercussions are still being felt today."

No one is certain today how rinderpest, an Asiatic bovine virus resembling measles, entered Africa. One theory suggests it was introduced by General Kitchener in 1884, when he herded Russian cattle from the Black Sea up the Nile as relief for the imperiled General Gordon in Khartoum. Another, more likely theory suggests the disease was introduced by the Italians when they imported Indian cattle during their invasion of Abyssinia (now Ethiopia) in 1889. The virus changed the face of eastern and southern Africa; by 1896 it had virtually decimated all the cattle in the Cape Province, some 3000 miles south of the Serengeti.

German explorer Oscar Baumann traveled through the Serengeti in 1891 and was struck particularly by rinderpest's effect upon the Masai themselves. He wrote: "A crowd of tattered scarecrows, now typical of the Masai country, gathered outside the thorn fence of our camp. There were women reduced to walking skeletons, out of whose sunken eyes looked the madness of hunger, children resembling deformed frogs rather than human beings, warriors who could scarcely crawl on all fours, and moronic, emaciated greybeards. These people ate everything available; dead donkeys were a delicacy for them; but they also devoured the skins, bones, and even horns of cattle. . . . They were refugees from the Serengeti, where starvation had depopulated whole districts."

Baumann probably never knew the word "rinderpest" and, in all likelihood, he could not diagnose smallpox, one of the side effects of famine. It is now believed that 95 percent of all cattle in East Africa perished. About the same proportion of wildebeest, buffalo, and, to a lesser extent, giraffe were also depleted. Rinderpest recurred in 1917–18, in 1923, between 1938 and 1941, and in 1957 and 1958. During this last outbreak, the Grzimeks began their historic flights across the Serengeti and estimated the wildebeest population at 99,481. At the time, they too were unaware that rinderpest had anything to do with the national park's population dynamics. In those days, the migration did not cross the border into Kenya. Still, the Grzimeks believed the migration, diminished as we now know, was one of the earth's wonders.

Today, in retrospect, scientists believe the Grzimeks' low-level transects and estimates might not have been accurate. Later censuses employed systematic photography and reflected counting errors. In 1962, after veterinarians had immunized cattle in the vulnerable areas at the edge of the park (note that the veterinarians' purpose was always the health of cattle, not of wild animals), rinderpest was virtually eliminated. Since then it has not been detected among the wildebeest of the Serengeti.

In 1962 wildebeest numbers were estimated at 250,000. By 1977, they had reached a peak of 1.4 million, a level which, by all

accounts, appears to be the capacity of the Serengeti-Mara eco-system. Buffalo numbers also increased but, possibly because wildebeest eat and trample much of the buffaloes' dry season food, the buffalo population wallowed in the early 1970s while the wildebeest's continued to increase. In 1982, with veterinarian services severely curtailed due to Tanzania's floundering economy, there was another outbreak of rinderpest, targeted this time specifically toward buffalo.

While buffalo populations have thus suffered a decline during the last few years, there have been no traces of rinderpest antibodies in blood samples from wildebeest. Possibly, commercial poaching on the outskirts of the park and drought conditions over the last three years are, in part, responsible for diminishing the herd's population by up to 100,000, but such losses are not what really bothers the scientists.

"The worst scenario I could imagine," says Dr. Borner, "is if rinderpest returned and reduced wildebeest numbers to, let's say, two hundred and fifty thousand. That part would be sad, but not tragic, as far as I'm concerned. The next sequence would represent the tragedy, for, no doubt, there'd be human population pressures—particularly in the north—to claim those areas of the park no longer occupied by wildebeest. And if we lost those lands, then the migration, as we know it now, would never, ever, be seen again."

Once a year, even during his late seventies, Dr. Bernhard Grzimek returned to Tanzania to place flowers on Michael's grave and to visit the Frankfurt Zoo's many projects in the Serengeti. He lost none of the enthusiasm he shared with his late son when they flew transects across what was then uncharted Africa. Alan Root, the film-maker, often joined doctors Borner and Grzimek on these trips, flying daringly as Michael once did. Root feels that the Serengeti migration exists, in great part, thanks to Dr. Grzimek's resolve. "Say what you will—you and I and a hundred others couldn't match the old man in what he's done for conservation. Nobody, in fact, can."

Nor is Alan Root being sentimental, for history relates that the Grzimeks drew the world's attention to the migration. They were the first conservationists to use airplanes to manage game. On his German television program, Bernhard Grzimek exhorted his countrymen to visit the Serengeti, and behind the scenes, with monies raised from his wildlife programs, he helped create the Serengeti Research Institute—a facility that today may be reborn.

Most remarkable of all was Dr. Grzimek's success in influencing the Tanzanian government to preserve the Serengeti. When he first met President Julius Nyerere, he noted the leader of this Third World nation's bafflement when told that Europeans would travel all the way to Africa merely to see an elephant. Today, nominally retired from office, Nyerere has become an ardent botanist and often he travels far just to see elephants. Not surprisingly, Tanzania, under his rule, contributed a greater percentage of national income to its parks than any western nation. "At one time," recalled Dr. Grzimek, "the Tanzanian government relocated several villages, just so the wildebeest migration would not be disturbed. Under the colonial administration such a move would have been considered outrageous."

Asked to sum up his remarkable career, Bernhard Grzimek steadied his faded blue eyes on a distant acacia tree. "I have fought all my life not for wild animals, but to preserve living rooms for wild animals. Nothing more."

And Serengeti today has come to be the very symbol of all such "living rooms." Flying east into steady rains with Alan Root, one is struck not just by that recurring sensation of timelessness but also by the notion that Serengeti means more than just a plain in Tanzania. In the sub-Arctic, up to 400,000 caribou trek annually from calving grounds to wintering pasture. In a remote corner of the southern Sudan, possibly three-quarters of a million white-eared kob annually file one by one from wetlands to grasslands. But only the wildebeest below our wingtips conduct such extravagant journeys on land that is of immediate appeal to agriculturists: Serengeti is an anomaly of our time.

"I think of lots of things when I watch them moving toward green grass," says Root, in answer to my question. "I think of 1840 Kansas, when three counties' worth of bison were so densely packed in the early mornings they formed their own cloud of fog overhead."

I paused to look down at the great shadow of wildebeest massing toward new grass and another season of life. I, too, thought of all the other great migrations that are no more—the wildebeest in Botswana, the hartebeest in Kenya. But especially I thought, like Alan, of those millions and millions of bison moving out across the Great Plains in my own country. I recalled that by the year 1900 only 500 out of many millions remained. The farmers and the ranchers had won. It is good, I began to think, for us humans to know we haven't been able to squash one really epic, last march. Ultimately, to watch another species forever bound for a new pasture has meaning far beyond the event.

A D V I S O R Y
The Best Way to See the Serengeti

Hardly any place in the world today can claim to have as many animals now as a century ago, but the abundance of wildlife in Tanzania's Serengeti Plains and Ngorongoro Crater is a wondrous exception. Probably the best time to visit the Serengeti is between the short rains of November/December and the long rains of April/May.

There are some interesting lodges in the Serengeti. Ndutu stands out among them for its rustic and personal atmosphere, and the much larger Lobo for its unique architecture—it is built into a huge rock outcropping overlooking the vast plain. (See "Where in

Africa?" page 7, for details.) But by far the best way to travel in Tanzania is on a customized or group tented safari. The food and service will be far superior to what you get in most lodges. Luxury under canvas can easily cost $300 to $500 per person per day; however, many adventure travel companies offer more basic but still comfortable tented safaris for quite a bit less.

Most trips to the Serengeti also include stays in Ngorongoro Crater, Lake Manyara, and sometimes Tarangire National Park. There's a lodge on the rim of the crater, but try to book a trip that includes camping on the crater floor—one of the best spots on the entire continent for seeing and hearing the sights and sounds of the African night.

Operators recommended for tented trips that include the Serengeti are:

ABERCROMBIE AND KENT INTERNATIONAL—THE MOST SUCCESSFUL A & K TRIPS TEND TO BE THE UPSCALE ONES. (1420 KENSINGTON ROAD, OAK BROOK, IL 60521; TEL. 800-323-7308 OR 312-954-2944)

EAST AFRICA SAFARI CO.—THIS BOOKING AGENCY, RUN BY MACKIE ARNSTEIN, WILL GIVE EXPERT ADVICE TO HELP YOU ARRANGE A PRIVATE TENTED SAFARI OR FIND AN APPROPRIATE GROUP TRIP, BUT YOU MAY END UP PAYING A BIT MORE. (250 WEST 57TH STREET, NEW YORK, NY 10017; TEL. 800-772-3214 OR 212-757-0722)

SPECIAL EXPEDITIONS—HEADED BY SVEN LIND-BLAD AND KNOWN FOR CAREFULLY PLANNED LUXURY GROUP TRIPS IN THE WILD. (720 FIFTH AVENUE, SUITE 605, NEW YORK, NY 10019; TEL. 800-762-0003 OR 212-765-7740) THEIR TENTED SAFARIS IN TANZANIA ARE ACTUALLY RUN BY THE UP-MARKET KENYAN OPERATOR KER AND DOWNEY.

KLR INTERNATIONAL—OFFERS A 16-DAY TANZANIA TENTED SAFARI FOR ABOUT $3000 PER PERSON. (1560 BROADWAY, SUITE 1308, NEW YORK, NY 10036; TEL. 212-869-2850)

OVERSEAS ADVENTURE TRAVEL—OAT OFFERS EQUALLY FASCINATING BUT LESS EXPENSIVE CAMPING SAFARIS IN TANZANIA. YOU'LL TRAVEL IN DUSTY, OPEN-SIDED BEDFORD TRUCKS AND YOU WON'T BE QUITE AS PAMPERED, BUT YOU'LL STILL BE WELL FED AND CARED FOR. BILLED AS "SOFT ADVENTURE," THESE TRIPS COST ONLY AROUND $180 PER PERSON PER DAY AND INCLUDE TWO NIGHTS IN LODGES.

FOR SLIGHTLY MORE, OAT RUNS A SPECIAL TWO-WEEK TRIP FOR 15 PEOPLE EVERY YEAR IN FEBRUARY, TIMED TO THE WILDEBEEST CALVING SEASON. GUIDED BY BEHAVIORAL ECOLOGIST DR. RICHARD ESTES OF HARVARD, WHO TEACHES A COURSE IN MAMMAL SOCIAL BEHAVIOR, THE TRIP FEATURES NIGHT-TIME TALKS AROUND THE CAMPFIRE BY ESTES AND OTHER SCIENTISTS WHO WORK IN THE SERENGETI. (349 BROADWAY, CAMBRIDGE, MA 02139; TEL. 617-876-0533 OR 800-221-0814)

WILDERSUN SAFARIS—BUDGET TRIPS LED BY TANZANIA SPECIALIST MERWYN NUNES. THE COST OF A 7-DAY LODGE AND TENT EXPEDITION IS ABOUT $700 PER PERSON. (BOX 930, ARUSHA, TANZANIA; TEL. 255-57-3880, TELEX 42126)

BJORN FIGENSHOU—A FULL TENTED SAFARI WITHOUT AIR CHARTERS IS ABOUT $300 PER PERSON PER DAY. (TANZANIA GUIDES, LTD., P.O. BOX 2031, ARUSHA, TANZANIA; TEL. 255-57-75-04; FAX 255-57-69-62)

DAVID PETERSON—HAS A GOOD KNOWLEDGE OF MASAI CULTURE. (DOROBO TOURS AND SAFARIS, BOX 2534, ARUSHA, TANZANIA; TEL. 255-57-2300, TELEX 42018)

DANNY MCCALLUM—THE MOST LUXURIOUS AND EXPENSIVE OF SERENGETI OPERATORS. DANNY HAS ADAPTED TECHNIQUES DISCOVERED AS A HUNTER TO THE PHOTOGRAPHIC SAFARI. EXPECT ORIENTAL RUGS IN YOUR TENTS, REFRIGERATORS IN EACH VEHICLE, STAPLES IMPORTED FROM BRITAIN. DECEMBER THROUGH MARCH AND JUNE (OLECHUGU SAFARIS, P.O. BOX 295, NANYUKI, KENYA; TEL. TIMAN 24; TELEX 25583; FAX 245-176-23416 AT NIGHT)

MASAI MARA CAMP

3

A SHORT WALK ACROSS MASAILAND

I WAS THE ONLY GUEST IN A LARGE TENT-ed hotel on the edge of Kenya's Masai Mara Game Reserve. Sunset had been accompanied by splinters of an electrical storm bolting across the plains, and now the pressure lamps had begun to attract swirling moths. A tented camp all to oneself is the height of self-indulgence, like being the only passenger on a great yacht. One of the many waiters clustered around the bar commented that the Talek River was rising once again; another remarked that where we were standing had been a foot under water last week. Thunder boomed and, far away, in response, a hyena yipped.

"Tomorrow," I said, "I plan to go walking. I'm looking for a Masai—someone who knows the country."

"I'll come." The speaker lounging by the bar was no Masai. Wearing shorts and a frayed khaki shirt, he had the features of a desert dweller—thin nose, clear copper skin, and well-traveled legs. He introduced himself as Gabriel Lawi, nineteen years old, a Samburu from near Maralal, 500 miles from here. "I have walked with *mzee juu*, Will-a-fred Thess-gear."

Wilfred Thesiger. As good as saying he had sailed with Sindbad. Thesiger was far and away Africa's most uncompromising walker. Born in the British legation in Addis Ababa, he came from English diplomatic stock. While at university he crossed Ethiopia's Danakil Depression—a first that solved the major Ethiopian geography conundrum—why the Awash River, rising in the mountains to the west of Addis, never reached the sea. He thereupon crossed Arabia's Empty Quarter—not once, but twice. Now, at the age of seventy, he regularly spent six months of each year trekking through the Northern Frontier of Kenya: a tall, hawk-nosed man, indifferent to most discomforts, hostile to European company except when contained within the walls of his London club. One hears that in waterless country he and his men materialize like apparitions, mirages, phantom caravans: two camels and four syces. I had met him on several occasions and always felt I was hobnobbing with someone of the ilk of T. E. Lawrence. Once, while waiting with him in his camp near Lake Turkana as the day cooled, he explained that he was not motivated merely by the walking, but by the desert people who accompanied him. Unspoiled Samburu were Thesiger's concept of aristocracy.

If Gabriel Lawi had been hired by Thesiger for a 2000-mile walk there was no doubt I could rely on him for a short jaunt of two days. Gabriel pulled a thorn from beneath his toenail and continued: "We call Thess-gear *mzee juu*——the old man always standing up ——because he can walk more than we can. He does not know how to stop. In the morning as we load the four jerricans of water on each camel he drinks big cups of coffee, and then all day walking without stop he drinks nothing, while we are all thirsty, and only at three when we stop will he drink again. *Mali mau* he calls it—— water with lemon and sugar——and maybe he will drink three, four, five glasses. He sits in his chair and says very little. Once, when it was so hot it melted skin, his eyes closed and his face went white, hanging down like this, with no breath from his lips. We were sure he was *kufa kabisa*——dead. But no. Suddenly, he stood up. 'Let's go,' he says. And we go, walking and walking."

The rain was now murmuring against the outer fly of the tent, and every ten minutes, when enough had accumulated in the loose folds of the canvas, a waiter poked a broom handle against the bulge to release a cascade onto the edge of the groundsheets. These were no ordinary rains——the short ones of November or the long rains of April and May. These were of epic dimensions, compared by old-timers to the deluge of 1961, when the Tana swelled to a width of three miles and the railbed of the Mombasa–Nairobi line was washed away. Last year the short rains had never ceased and four additional deluvian months had gate-crashed into the start of the year. Throughout much of Kenya the ground was awash, just the tips of the grass stems peering above the level of the flood. I had heard that in the north of the country the Chalbi Desert, once a salty cauldron, now resembled an English cutting garden, and everywhere tourists were stranded; minibuses washed over drifts and even airfields had vanished into the flood plains of rivers. The news had been too much for some New York friends who had planned to join me on this five-day walk across Masailand. "I don't mind walking," one of them had said, "but not at the risk of drowning."

I was first stung by Africa in 1960. I was sixteen then and Africa seemed young, too. I like to think we grew up together——I was first a watcher, then a hunter, and now again a watcher. And during this time Africa underwent not just a change in taste, but a change in identity——once it was a pupa, now it's emerged a moth.

My one constant in Africa has been its bushland. Of course, it's been greatly reduced since 1960, but these days when it's good, it's just as it was when I was sixteen and I am suffused by those long-ago smells and sounds. Now, usually pressed for time, I find a good walk is often the most satisfying way to compress the best of Africa into the shortest space of time. One year I backpacked 100 miles through the Kedong Valley. This year I would begin another walk, starting from Fig Tree Camp, on the edge of the Masai Mara, and looping farther and farther into the adjoining land.

I am no stranger to the Mara, but in the past I have had to content myself with watching game strictly from the car. Outside the reserve, game laws have no muscle and the game wanders willy-nilly in and out of the protected areas. By walking close to the boundaries one is likely to see almost as much game outside the reserve as within.

There I would no doubt also encounter Masai trailing their cattle, living in their biodegradable fortresses, called *manyattas*.

The next morning I stood scratching and shivering at the river. Lawi had brought along Kipeng, the Masai nightwatchman, a much taller man whose earlobes had been perforated to carry tins of snuff. Now, without time to find a container, he had knotted each lobe into a granny knot.

Heavy clouds like bunches of raw cotton gathered from out of the east for a turn at ramming the Siria Escarpment. Lawi would have nothing to do with predictions, and Kipeng made it clear that he was superior to rain or drought. I posed for a photograph with the umbrella—an opéra-bouffe imperialist, served by faithful retainers. Nonetheless, I was not exuding confidence and Lawi, I could tell, was not confident of his new leader, having walked to the ends of the earth with the great Thess-gear. "Are you ready?" he asked haltingly.

The first step of a long walk is always the most self-conscious. It takes a thousand times longer than any subsequent step, and it hurts in a way that has nothing to do with pain. In a while, the step was complete and when my sandals had become comfortable, the mud forming itself to my instep, my toes squirming for a foothold, I felt springlike, floating. The mud crept up to my ankles and soon there were dark brushstrokes of earth across my shorts. After an hour, walking requires absolutely no more awareness until the very last hour before sunset when a knee begins to jerk or a blister develops on a toe. In between, no conscious effort is required; foot follows foot of its own accord, and almost all activity while padding along takes place in the mind.

Our route lay in a direct line to a Masai *manyatta* and then south into a range of hills, looping to the west and then back along the Talek to Fig Tree Camp. It's fruitless to estimate mileage in this country, where the shortest route between two points is very often an arc. By the end of the day we blithely decreed we had covered sixteen miles. Another sixteen would not have been beyond our capacity, for the mud was firm and the air, for Africa, cool. Once the steady pace is mastered in this rough country, it is troubling to pause; the plunging beat of one's heart commands the feet to its rhythm.

"Sopa, ero." The Masai make little of a stranger who addresses them in their language. Nor were these *morani*, warriors, surprised to see me loping cross-country bound for the beyond. They expected us to stop as they leaned one-legged against their spears. For a while it was not certain if they intended more than a stare. Their ochre-red cloaks, hanging from their shoulders, sometimes covered them, sometimes didn't. Coils of copper ran through their ears, and occasionally a gust of wind would indelicately catch a cloak, exposing everything, including angry thigh wounds caused by lions, spears, broken branches—Masai bravura.

"Ask him," I said to Kipeng, "why all Masai demand money whenever a traveler asks to take their picture."

The dialogue between my second-in-command and the becloaked *moran* seemed to be a mean-spirited exchange of insults ending with a few explosive sounds as if both Masai were gagging on pits.

I laughed back.

"Because," the *moran* replied at last, "when you take pictures it sucks blood from us."

"When I take this picture of a 'Tommie,'" I countered, "you tell me whether you can see the blood drained from him." I duly snapped a shot of a nearby Thomson gazelle. The Masai said nothing.

"If the camera did suck blood from you," I continued, "you should not allow anyone to take a picture of you at any price . . . But, as you can see, photography is quite harmless."

The *moran* stuck the butt of his spear into the ground. The truth was on its way. "You see," he said finally, "when the first white man came here he offered us money for our pictures. So now we must ask all other white men."

I gagged and soon we all were laughing. "*Osirian*," I said. "Good-bye."

"*Osirian.*" We five little spots on a buff plain, once clustered together, now drew apart—two walking west, three east—and the game soon began to graze where we had collected, and across all this continuity other gazelles loped from tussock to clump, with only the barest concept of destination.

Ours was the Masai *manyatta* on the far side of a fast-rushing stream with a slippery bottom. Once inside the cluster of dung huts, the texture and color of fresh brownies, we were invited to retrace our steps across the stream to join the elders for a feast. A sheep had been slaughtered and already a thin vein of smoke was hopscotching across the sky. When we arrived at the clearing the elders were squatting by the fire, as wiry dogs sniffed at the head of the sheep, its eyes still open. I was greeted by the old men as if I had been expected. The mutton was tough as peeled bark, but I mimicked them and smacked my lips and tried not to look at the sheep's head.

My field glasses excited their wonder. Crowing with laughter, they scrutinized the faces of their companions. When I finally retrieved the glasses I noticed that a peculiar Masai skin tonic, made from animal fat, now covered the lenses.

These old men, unlike the young, clothed themselves in heavy blankets against the rain. All suffered from eye disease. One man had only a socket; many of the others walked with care, for a blue film covered their irises. Watching them huddled by the fire, their knotted hands probing the fire for more meat, I realized they had probably witnessed both the beginning and the end of imperialism in Kenya. "Who was the first white man you ever met?" I asked.

"In the beginning," the oldest replied, "there were only four white men: Corpe, Musitet, Cole, and Delamere." I recognized only the last two: the Earl of Enniskillen and Lord Delamere, both of whom settled in Kenya during the early days of the colony at the beginning of the century.

"Is it true you Masai stole many of Delamere's cattle?"

A gag of laughter. "It was not us. It was *other* Masai." Now they all rattled with laughter, for cattle-stealing can be a joke.

"And Lynn Temple-Borham—did you know him?"

"T-B," as he was known by all, had been the game warden of the Masai Mara for many years. I had met him shortly before his sudden death and, like all who knew him, had considered him one of the last great gents of the bush. He had created this reserve in large part thanks to the high esteem in which he was held by the Masai.

The old men clicked to show their approval. I was expecting to hear something elegiac. "His wife," an old man began, "she was deaf."

"But did you Masai give him land—you who never willingly give your land away, especially to a *mzungu*, a white man?" Surely they would let loose with some praise. I had idolized "T-B" because he had set such a prescient standard for white-Masai relations.

"Because he begged for it."

I felt robbed. "But wasn't it because he had done so much for the Masai?"

"Yes. He brought medicines to our villages. Best of all, he protected us from the Kikuyu. That was in the time of Mau Mau."

Mau Mau. Even in Kenya today, it is easy to overlook the Mau Mau Emergency. It has been eclipsed by Kasavubu's Congo, Idi Amin's Uganda, Mengistu's Ethiopia, and pre-independence Rhodesia. Yet, here in Kenya during the 1950s, the Kikuyu hamstrung, dismembered, eviscerated, castrated, and butchered nearly 20,000 people who did not take their oath. Hundreds of Masai were slaughtered as innocent victims of a war being waged far to the east. I have always been surprised that the British, lionizers of the Masai and their independent ways, should have abandoned them so totally at independence in 1963. Surely they should have left behind some structure that would have guaranteed them their civil rights in a country being handed over to their traditional enemies.

I looked once again at the sheep's head. The oldest man nodded for me to follow. We recrossed the river and, on all fours, entered

his hut. The interior, dark and warm, was divided into four rooms. A very young calf was stashed in one; in another only a broken stool—the air still gritty from last night's fire. The old man explained that ten people slept here regularly, their bodies so tight-pressed that even a thin snake could not slip through the knot of humanity. A calabash of milk was passed to me. It was sweet and smoky; in the darkness I could not see if it had been mixed with cow's blood.

"Are you still angry," I inquired, "that the white man stole your land and handed it over to the Kikuyus?"

"No," the old man said after a pause. "It is forgotten. But . . ."

I pretended to drink some more milk.

"But if he takes our land again, we will fight."

A woman entered. Her head was shaved and some of her lower teeth had been chipped out. Her neck seemed unnaturally long because of three beaded collars; holes had been pierced through the tops of her ears to allow for still another cascade of beadwork. She giggled at me, half clucking, half humming. Suddenly a torrent of words spilled through her ragged teeth. Kipeng laughed.

"What does she say?"

"She wants to know whether you want to sleep with her now?"

By now the day had grown warm, and walking in a southwesterly direction brought us into alternate patches of shade and sunshine. Around the Masai *manyattas* the grass was low and only Thomson gazelles, tails flicking like metronomes, exploited the marginal grazing. But as the *manyattas* were left behind, the grass grew higher, leaving droplets of water high on our legs. The game was now in great numbers, insulated from us by only the briefest *cordon sanitaire*. The topi, antelope that seem to wear rugby socks, scrutinized us and then, reassured we were only white Masai, hobbled a token distance to resume their grazing. The game seemed to have read the official gazette, which prohibited all hunting throughout the country; at times we could approach to within 50 meters of impala, giraffe, and kongoni. Pygmy mongooses, called *katetes*, had settled in air vents of a termite mound and nattered breezily as we passed.

I tripped. "Sorry," Lawi and Kipeng said simultaneously. They had been talking together in ki-Masai and now Lawi hung back worried. It was clear he had considered me imprudent to turn down the Masai lady's generous offer. "And when a child," he began, "is born out of marriage in your country, what happens to the children?"

"First a question: Are many children born out of marriage amongst the Masai and the Samburu?"

"Yes. It can happen any time after a girl is thirteen."

"And?"

"Just the girl takes the child. It is normal and everyone is happy."

"Well, in America the child is often put up for adoption."

"Adoption?"

"It means the child is taken to a special home where there are many other children without parents, and strangers may come and when they see a child they like they may take it home to be brought up as their own."

Lawi walked ahead moodily.

"What's bothering you?"

"This is terrible. I do not like this custom in America."

Soon we were amid the hills and our course was veering more and more to the west. Streambeds that had been dry for many years had now burst their sides and the only way to negotiate their deep muddy bottoms was to remove *chopplis* (sandals), balance them, cameras, wallet, and sandwiches on our heads. Once out of the rivers, our clothes dried quickly and all that was left to remind us of these river crossings was a muddy high-water mark near the shoulders of our shirts.

An hour before sunset we padded into Fig Tree, our lunch sandwiches still forgotten. On many of my other walks, a day's destination would often be a good shade tree, never a luxurious tented camp. There, before dusk, we would scramble to find dry kindling and as night spread, our fire would splutter to life. My bed would be a canvas groundsheet, and often I treated myself to a thimble of whiskey for company with the stars. In only a matter

of moments Africa would become a haunted land, the light from our puny fire a cozy cave chiseled out of the dark.

Did Thesiger feel the same? Did he delight in the evening murmur of voices, rising and falling out of the wail of the night? No doubt he would have raised his eyebrows at the sight of Fig Tree Camp. Far too clean and well lighted for the Africa he fancied. Being made of less stern stuff, I found the long row of green tents very appealing. I was not tired, but my knee was playing up and, anyway, for the last hour I had been daydreaming about a plunge in the river.

Arrival at Fig Tree coincided with that of twenty-two American military advisers traveling incognito in an air-conditioned Mercedes bus. When I reached them, they were gravely watching the river, trying to suppress the occasional salute. "Does your presence here have anything to do with the recent sale of the F-16s to the Kenyan Air Force?" I inquired. A double bourbon fell to the ground, and after an unpleasant silence I jumped into the river, saving myself from traveling downstream next to a bloated kongoni carcass by use of a line tied to the taproots of a fig tree. Opaque and inviting as chocolate, this river was the supreme reward. Pity about all these new guests. No doubt these military advisers shared my sentiment. Whenever I surfaced I saw a row of high-ranking heads looking disappointed that crocs were in short supply.

In the morning, glad to be away from all the guarded talk of African detente, I set off for my final walk, this time led by Miles Burton, the camp's owner. Accompanied again by Lawi, we drove northwest for nearly an hour and, upon reaching a hill that resembled a monk's shaved head, we jumped out of the Land Cruiser and bade the driver farewell. We would now return to camp along a different route. For a while we waited for the silence to gather about us and for a pale chanting goshawk to launch itself from an acacia. While it hesitated, Miles began discussing with Lawi our proposed route back to camp. He too spotted the authority of this nineteen-year-old Samburu. Both had probably spent the same number of years in the bush and shared much in common. Dressed

in shorts, his legs burned and scratched, Miles was a burly En-
glishman who seemed always to be pushing his body to extremes.
His short-sleeved shirt had once been long-sleeved, his binoculars
were chipped, and his tattered khaki hat could not contain tussocks
of bleached hair. One could imagine that Miles might have been
more robust had he not spent the better part of his life walking.

"It'll happen," he said, glassing the hills in search of buffalo.
"Tourists just can't stand being pulled around by the nose. They
want to see game on foot, get away from the bloody minibuses.
Kenya is catering to a bunch of bum-sitters. They sit on their bums
in the buses. They sit on their bums in the hotels. Might as well
get them wheelchairs. And you know, they don't like it one bit.
They want to get out. They just don't dare ask."

Miles hoped to lead this rebellion from motorized transport.
His safaris would be called "a walk through Masailand," and they
would last for five days, starting at the Siria Escarpment and ending
on the Talek River, all within a few short miles of the reserve
boundary. On foot there would be time to notice the convolution
of an elephant's ear, the royal chamber of a termite mound, the
lion heart of an ant lion. Each day camps would be portaged ahead
of the walkers by a special vehicle, and by midday there would be
cool drinks and shade awaiting the walkers.

As soon as we made our first footstep we heard a hum out of
the west. "Get down," Miles yelled, and as we did a swarm of
bees passed overhead, pulsing like high-tension wire. "You see,"
he remarked, "had you been in a car you wouldn't have noticed.
Or cared."

In other circumstances quick with a laugh, on a foot safari Miles
said little. Chatter, he explained, could ruin a walkabout. On foot
one must engage oneself in a listening game. You ask a question,
you make a quick observation and, when done, embalm yourself
in sounds.

We walked for most of the morning, and shortly before we
reached camp Miles spotted a herd of buffalo. Since they were
grazing in heavy bush we approached to within a hundred feet.

And when they still did not notice, we crept closer, both of us acting as if we carried a gun instead of two sets of field glasses. It became a game of wits: How close could we get? At fifty feet, the wind veered and the buffaloes' heads swung mightily and then they bucked and surged, crashing through the underbrush until they were out of sight. I smelled their sweat and their dust crept over us. A prickle set my neck to itching: This was the moment that had drawn me years before to hunting.

"You know," I said to Miles, "Lawi used to walk with Wilfred Thesiger."

Miles studied him, his slight figure moving through the grass with less pretension than a wild animal. Lawi stopped.

"Thesiger is getting old now," Miles said to him.

"Old yes, but he does not want to die."

For an hour we walked in silence. Soon I came to hear the pinking of the camp's diesel generator. Perhaps, after all, two days of walking is not enough: I still felt comfortable with the sound of a piston engine. On a real walk, far from roads and canvas, even the whine of a distant airplane can become a calamity.

When we reached a bush track, we noticed an approaching Land Rover. We studied it through the glasses, as if it were a herd of buffalo. And all the while we were being scrutinized by its occupants. It seemed we were the anomaly. The car came to a halt and three heads, emerging through the roof hatch, watched us suspiciously. Miles cleared his throat. "*Konnen sie*," he said, affecting a German accent, "tell me ze vay *zum* ze lodge, *bitte?*"

"The lodge?" responded the American driver. "Jeez, it's miles from here."

"*Ja*, our motorkaa vas stuk in ze river last abent and ve haf been valking since dis morgen."

"Oh, my God. We'll give you a lift."

"*Nein*, zis is *nicht* necessaire. Ve shall valk."

"But the lodge is at least twenty miles from here."

"No matter. Vick vay, *bitte?*"

"Over there." The tourist pointed high on the horizon, not

knowing that our real destination was Fig Tree Camp, hidden in the trees not even a mile from here.

"Zat is *gut. Danke.*"

"We have oranges," they pleaded.

"*Nein, nicht* necessaire." We resumed our walk and for a while the Americans trailed us in reverse.

"Please, can't we give you a lift?"

"*Nein*, ve like zis valking."

At last, with all their arguments exhausted, they came to a halt. "Loonies," I heard them say.

I wondered how Thesiger would have behaved.

A D V I S O R Y

Getting Out of the Car in East Africa

Hakara hakara haina baraka.
("In hurry hurry there is no blessing.")

Pole pole ndiyo mwendo.
("Slowly slowly is indeed the proper path.")

—Swahili proverbs

For the visitor to East Africa who heeds this Swahili advice, the "proper path" just might be a walking tour. It's an ideal way to slow down and absorb more. In contrast to Zimbabwe and Zambia, where foot safaris are offered at practically every lodge and camp and by a host of independent operators, Kenya and Tanzania have not traditionally been considered "getting out of the car" places. But East African safari operators are beginning to offer more opportunities to see the country at a slower pace—on horseback, by boat, and even by camel, as well as on foot.

Here are some ways for the adventurous traveler to experience the wildlife of Kenya and Tanzania up close:

- WITH UP TO 30 PORTERS, 6 TO 8 PEOPLE CAN WALK INTO THE HEART OF TANZANIA'S VAST AND UNSPOILED SELOUS GAME RESERVE WITH **RICHARD BONHAM**, THE RECOGNIZED AUTHORITY ON THIS GREAT WILDERNESS. YOU'LL TRAVEL ON FOOT AND BY BOAT, ENCOUNTERING HIPPO, ELEPHANTS, LIONS, AND BUFFALO. A 14-DAY TRIP COSTS ABOUT $6,100. BONHAM ALSO OFFERS WALKS IN KENYA'S CHYULU HILLS NEAR AMBOSELI. (BOOK THROUGH SAFARI CONSULTANTS OF LONDON, 3535 RIDGELAKE DRIVE, SUITE B, METAIRIE, LA 70002; TEL. 800-648-6541.)

- YOU CAN APPROACH ANIMALS FROM THE WATER, WHERE THEY LEAST EXPECT YOU, FROM A BOAT THAT FLOATS DOWN EAST AFRICA'S LARGEST RIVER, THE RUFIJI, NEAR THE SELOUS GAME RESERVE. OPERATOR **CONRAD HIRSH** OFFERS THIS 17-DAY TRIP FOR AROUND $3,500 PER PERSON IN DECEMBER, JANUARY, JUNE, AND JULY ONLY. ACCOMMODATIONS ARE ELEMENTAL, BUT YOU'LL SEE AFRICA AS IT ONCE WAS. (BOOK THROUGH SOBEK EXPEDITIONS, INC., BOX 1089, ANGELS CAMP, CA 95222; TEL. 209-736-4524.)

- THE DRY DESERT PLAINS OF KENYA'S SPARSELY POPULATED NORTH ARE IDEAL FOR CAMEL SAFARIS. THEY CARRY THE SUPPLIES WHILE YOU WALK WITH GUIDE **SIMON EVANS** OVER THE SEVERE AND BEAUTIFUL TERRAIN. VIEW DESERT GAME AND MEET THE SAMBURU PEOPLE. $100 A DAY, INCLUDING DELICIOUS THREE-COURSE MEALS. (BOOK THROUGH JUST THE TICKET, BOX 14845, NAIROBI, KENYA; TEL. 254-2-741755.)

- THOUGH **PETER JONES** SPECIALIZES IN ANTHROPOLOGICAL SAFARIS, HE ALSO LEADS WALKING AND DRIVING TRIPS IN THE SERENGETI, NGORONGORO CRATER, AND THE OLDUVAI GORGE. THE COST DEPENDS ON THE SIZE

OF THE GROUP AND DEGREE OF LUXURY. (BOX 49, ARU-
SHA, TANZANIA; TEL. 255-57-7803)

• ANNE KENT TAYLOR, WHO OFTEN LIVES ON A MON-
TANA RANCH, ORGANIZES AND WILL ACCOMPANY SMALL
GROUPS ON CUSTOMIZED HORSEBACK OR WALKING SA-
FARIS TO OFF-THE-BEATEN TRACK LOCATIONS WITH RICH-
ARD BONHAM, TONY CHURCH, OR PETER JONES. (CONTACT
HER AT A. K. TAYLOR INTERNATIONAL, 2724 ARVIN ROAD,
BILLINGS, MT 59102; TEL. 406-656-0706.)

• EQUITOUR, BASED IN WYOMING, BOOKS HORSEBACK/
CAMPING SAFARIS TO KENYA. OWNERS BAYARD AND MEL
FOX FREQUENTLY JOIN STOUT-HEARTED RIDERS ON
EQUITOUR'S 15-DAY "KENYA ENDURANCE SAFARI,"
WHERE ALL TRAVEL IS ON HORSEBACK, OR THE MORE
RELAXED 16-DAY "KENYA COMBINATION RIDE," WHERE
DAYS ON HORSEBACK ARE INTERSPERSED WITH GAME-
VIEWING BY VEHICLE ($3850/PERSON). MOST TRIPS ARE
LED BY TONY CHURCH, A 20-YEAR VETERAN OPERATOR
OF HORSEBACK SAFARIS ON THE OUTSKIRTS OF KENYA'S
MASAI MARA. (EQUITOUR, P.O. BOX 807, DUBOIS, WY
82513; TEL. 800-545-0019.)

GABRIEL LAWI NOW WALKS VERY INFREQUENTLY SINCE
HE WAS RECENTLY ELECTED MAYOR OF MARALAL. SADLY,
MILES BURTON, DEAN OF WALKING SAFARIS, WAS KILLED
A YEAR AFTER I WALKED WITH HIM.

(For a list of guides who organize walks that focus exclusively on the people and cultures of East Africa, see "Advisory: How to Walk into the Stone Age," in Chapter 12, "Traipsing Through Time," page 221.)

The Iron Snake

4

SHAKEDOWN ON THE IRON SNAKE

"An Iron Snake will cross from the lake of salt to the lands of the Great Lake."

—19th-century African prophecy

THE TRAIN IS NOT A GIMMICK, I INSISTED

with about as much integrity as a sideshow barker. The chilled Dom Perignon at eight in the morning—fair enough. But not the train. No, the Iron Snake is a sensible creation. It was conceived simply to transport tourists through East Africa. Because it will serve as a kind of movable hotel, nothing could be more practical.

Aha: Here is where Geoffrey Kent, Jorie Butler, the East African Railroad Corporation, and I, smiling deliriously, parted company with common sense. Take a closer look at the Iron Snake, marshalling its strength in the Nairobi Station. No everyday train. This is a rolling pleasure palace. Steam hisses at pressure points from each of the four immaculately polished carriages, and beneath the boiler of the 150-ton locomotive called "Nyatura" (after a tribe in Tanzania) there is an incandescence as bright as the sun over Africa. Everything about it speaks of a long-ago time. The engine was specially selected, for it is guaranteed never to exceed 35 miles an hour (promise). The carriages seem even older—artifacts from the days when luxurious travel was not a red-eyed rush from one time zone to another. The cars are from the gilded age of travel. Years ago they grew old and were mothballed. They had been designed to take railroad directors and VIPs (including the Prince of Wales) through the country; today they have been superseded by a tight seat in an overcrowded airplane. Luckily, far-seeing executives in the EARC maintained them, and today, February 20, 1976, they have been reborn with all the hoopla of the opening of the Union Pacific.

The time is 8:05. Reporters, white hunters, and nonbelievers crowd the platform. Brown Waweru, the railroad's traffic manager, watches his creation with pride. Thompson Brown, the chief catering officer, gives last-minute instructions to one of his expert cabin attendants regarding the exact millimetric distance the sheets must be turned down. Bouquets of red roses and white carnations are brought to each of the cabins by a team of men with smiles as large as Mombasa Harbor. In the dining cars, silverware that has not been used since the days of the now-defunct Uganda Railroad is being polished and laid out with a diamond cutter's skill. (Imagine: three different kinds of forks!) And in the saloon car the leather chairs and the oak-paneled walls are being rubbed with a lemon compound until they glow like horse chestnuts.

8:10: The engineer, already covered in petroleum, prods the coupling, and the brakeman inspects the grease boxes over each set of wheels. At the rear of the train a brake van has been attached, and it should be any minute now that we leave.

8:13: With only two minutes to go, our guests arrive. Suitcases swirl. Solar topis are distributed. James Niven, David's son, sees the train for the first time. "I didn't bring my camera for a very good reason. I just want to enjoy the view." Alix Plum, having just dedicated a school in Botswana with Neil McConnell, gasps and giggles. "You know, I think if Roy [her husband] had known it was going to be this plush, he would have come, too." Several professional hunters, gargling on the champagne, are sure the train will never leave the station. "Mombasa is that way," one of them splutters. "Rubbish," the other chimes in. "I thought you'd know something after eighty years in the business. It's thataway" (pointing to Lake Naivasha).

8:20: The public address system crackles: "The special train on track number one is five minutes late in departing for Mombasa."

8:45: In the saloon car three bartenders are all-hands as they decork, and fine crystal is being passed through the open windows. An antique poster has been unearthed to decorate the interior. It reads: "The Highlands of British East Africa: A Winter Home for

Aristocrats." Below it a cartoon shows an alleged aristocrat sup-
plicating a man-eater at the Nairobi Station while dirty-dhotied
Babus flee before a gaggle of elephants, pythons, and hippos. Again
the loudspeakers hiss: "The special train on track number one is
now a half hour late."

"This is what Africa's all about," a white hunter says. "Learn
to love it."

"You don't have to convince me," Jack Heminway replies.

8:52: "Would you mind going aboard please?" A Pullman porter
could learn something from this man, the most polite steward I
ever met. Our twenty-three staff members are all on the platform,
checking that there are no malingerers. "All aboard." Like an old
gentleman gliding between the tables at Le Tour d'Argent, the
Iron Snake leaves Nairobi. Children gathered along the embank-
ments ululate and wave.

The champagne splashes in the tulip glasses as we cross switch-
overs, the train slowly gathering speed for a wild straight dash into
Athi River. We are all of forty-five minutes late arriving at our
first stop, but the only person who notices this arithmetic is our
engineer, who must now restructure our running schedule if we
are to coordinate with other traffic on the rails. Kenya's 800 miles
of track are a single-line system, hardly changed since they were
first laid down after 1896. (One notable change has been the
addition of rock ballast underneath the tracks. Before that it was
every colonial child's pleasure to arrive at school off the train
covered in a thick coat of red dust.) Since there is a steady coming
and going of freight trains, our engineer will have to establish that
the run between each station siding is clear of other traffic before
he can proceed. At each siding he relays to the stationmaster a
key strapped to a birch and leather harness. This, in effect, is his
key to the next stretch of track, and it must be inserted by the
stationmaster into an antique brass switching transformer in the
station house to clear the way.

Six Masai gathered on the siding at Athi River did not let the
Iron Snake's arrival interrupt their contemplation of the scrubby

grasslands. "Pikshas," they repeated after us, as though they had never heard the word before. A thin stream of brown spittle shot from one *moran*'s mouth, and with his sinewy hand he rubbed the sun and the flies from his eyes. No doubt he was implying we could not afford his price.

Daphne Hainworth, fresh from the Old Master's Department at Sotheby's in London, had been met just in time at the airport this morning by an Abercrombie and Kent car, and rushed here to meet us. Beautifully pale, she bubbled with triumphs and scandals and revelations from that other universe. She passed around the latest London newspapers. "That's great," someone said.

"There's Lukenya to the north," Alan Price said, trying to divert the conversation to more important matters.

The train stations after Athi River read like a chronicle of early colonial history: Stoney Athi, Kapiti Plains, Sultan Hamud, Kiboko (meaning "hippo" or "whip"), and Darajani. In the saloon car all the windows are open and the overhead fan puts a sting in the wind. "Far better than air conditioning," says Porter Ijams, the thirteenth best backgammon player in the world. "Somebody once knew how to live."

"Kima." I see the one-room station hurtling past us. In Swahili it means "mincemeat," and no wonder, for here the great colonial experiment ran into a "spot of bother." It happened in June 1900, when a fellow named Ryall, a young superintendent of police fresh from England, was sharing his hospitality in an inspection coach on the siding with two traders—an Italian and a German. Ryall had been posted to stand guard between midnight and three, but he must have fallen asleep with the door slightly ajar. In the blackness outside, a great lion had been watching. Slowly it crept up on the carriage, slipped through the door, spotted Ryall on the lower bunk, failed to notice the Italian trader asleep on the floor, leaped onto the lower bunk, and closed his jaws around poor Ryall's head.

Ryall is today buried in Nairobi, and the outline of his unhappy

end is fully documented on his headstone, as was the custom in Victorian times. What is not told in the cemetery is that when the lion leaped onto Ryall's bunk, the open door through which it had entered slid shut, locking carnivore, German, Italian, and struggling Ryall together in the very small room. The lion's rear feet, it seemed, were firmly planted on the Italian's back while the German jumped off the top bunk onto the lion and then bolted for the washroom. Several minutes must have elapsed before the lion, reversing with his prey in his mouth, discovered that the door was now firmly shut and his only exit would have to be through a small window. Fortunately for the Italian, the man-eater could only deal with one white man at a time. It wedged itself through the window and loudly finished Ryall off a few feet from the footplate, much to the discomfort of his Italian and German guests, who were unable to get back to sleep.

"Three Tommies!" We all peer out of the windows, not because Thomson gazelle are rareties, but because game is, after all, the object of the Iron Snake. We are still about thirty miles from Tsavo National Park, but all the large ranches to either side of the tracks are teeming with game—zebra, impala, and Grant's gazelle. Incredibly, few animals raise their heads to see us pass. Even cattle herders have the courtesy to take a passing interest in our rumbling passage, but not the game. The "Tommies" graze peacefully within twenty feet of the rails, tails flicking, their eyes bent to the yellowing stubble. Of course, the big excitement will be to see elephant and rhino. Perhaps these may react differently. In the early days, when rhinos were not programmed to view the railroad with equanimity, one actually had the bad manners to charge a locomotive. Somewhere now in Rhino Heaven there is a pig-eyed angel gleefully singing: "I nicked the boiler . . . I nicked the boiler."

Giraffes occasionally cause a nuisance even now when they run pell mell across the tracks, coiling the copper telegraph wires around their necks.

There is no doubt the game has decreased slightly since 1902, when Colonel R. Meinertzhagen made the following count from his carriage window in a twenty-two-mile stretch just before he reached Nairobi: "5 rhinoceros, 18 giraffe, 760 wildebeests, 4006 zebra, 845 Coke's hartebeeste, 324 Grant's gazelle, 142 Thomson gazelle, 46 impala, 24 ostrich, 7 great bustard and 16 baboon." So far we can match him on most species (but not numbers) except for rhinoceros. Through some trees I can spot three giraffes and, on the middle of a plain, a secretary bird struts. We are now "one up" on Meinertzhagen. "Four ostrich," Neil McConnell shouts. We are catching up fast, but I can see we will run into trouble with the 845 Coke's hartebeeste. Chimes sound from the length of the corridor. Our chief steward, Mr. Stephen Mutua, is playing "reveille," and our group of thirteen filter into the two dining rooms to discover that what was billed as a light cold lunch consists of a citrus fruit basket, consommé royale, one gigantic baked ham, an enormous sirloin of beef, stuffed egg mayonnaise, saffron rice with curry, chicken pie, breast of chicken with supreme sauce, crumbed fish tartare, liver pâté, ox tongue with white sauce, eight different kinds of salad, apple pie with custard sauce, Charlotte Russe, and an assortment of cheeses so diverse that even the Galloping Gourmet would be reduced to a slow walk.

The menu was remarkable by itself, but what seemed so improbable was its proximity to that gliding view of the Chyulu Hills looking like toy soldiers at the ankles of distant Kilimanjaro. And everywhere we looked now: game. It was absurd to enjoy this immense land in an oak-paneled carriage with Mr. Francis Rujumba, Mr. Stephen Mutua, Mr. George Githome, and Mr. Mwilu Mutua all insisting I sample the port. "Decadent," said Armene Norris, of New York. "Decadent," repeated Gini Semenenko, of Boston. "I'll have seconds on the Charlotte Russe," I said.

At 4:07 in the afternoon there was a cry from a bathroom. Norah Knott had been amusing herself in the bathtub, watching the water splash in rhythm to the clicking of the rails. Suddenly she let out a scream. She had left her window completely open and, within twenty feet of where she bathed, an elephant had come into view and then disappeared. By the time it shunted past

the windows in the saloon car, it was rubbing its bottom against a thorn tree, oblivious of our passage. Nothing but a tick was going to disturb its midafternoon "kip."

After braking to a halt in Mbinzau, I came across a startling human adaptation. A horde of Wakamba women, draped in spanking clean Mother Hubbards, clustered about the engine with pots and calabashes. It was second nature for them to find a certain spigot mounted under the boiler. Abuse simmering with laughter, they jostled each other, waiting their turn to fill up. "They're getting boiling water without having to heat it," I suggested. The engineer knew better.

"Not hot water," he said. "Water . . . in Mbinzau there's no water at all. Not a water hole for miles. The loco is their only source."

At sunset we reached Mtito Ndei, where we would "stable" for the night. We decided on a walk to the Tsavo Inn and, armed only with bathing suits, we made our way down a dirt road, past an outpost of the African Inland Mission, where dogs barked and singsong babble from the smoky huts mixed with the belch of tree frogs. The swim in the pool under the Southern Cross could only have been improved had it been in the Athi River; and later dinner on the Iron Snake even surpassed lunch. By eleven, spoiled, self-indulged, and slightly gorged, we listened to that antique sound of fans slicing the cool night air, and Alan Price's voice melodiously telling an awed audience of a rhino he had once known called "Sidney." Sidney had lived in a valley near here, and every time Alan had driven into the valley Sidney had charged the car. Whenever Sidney did not charge, Alan began to worry about Sidney. "Come on, Sidney old boy, let's have a little of the old 'what have you.'" And sure enough, Sidney would find those words so menacing that he would lower his head and come thundering at the car. Last year Alan had driven into the valley and could not find Sidney. He looked and looked and finally came across Sidney's mummified carcass beside a dry water hole—a victim of the drought. "I don't like going back to that valley now. It's terrible losing an enemy."

At dawn the next day our train was met by a squadron of Abercrombie and Kent cars, and until two in the afternoon we fanned out in all directions, some of us going as far as Voi, others to Mzima Springs to watch the hippos trot through clear water and crocodiles feed on barbus.

15:30. I open the side-door in one of the saloon cars, after another Cordon Bleu lunch, and prop myself in a leather chair to watch the copper-colored brachiastegia brush glide past. Elephants, buffalo, a distant rhino darken the sparse shade, and a small herd of giraffe run away at a gentle angle, their necks coiling and snapping like ocean breakers. The train has a wonderful way of minding its own business, and the game seems to know it. We are just another pachyderm, charging down a predictable path, bent on just as prehistoric a thought as those giants dozing in the shade.

A slight decline and twist in the tracks tell me we are about to cross the Tsavo River. Here seventy-eight years ago Lt. Col. J. H. Patterson and about a thousand Indian coolies were given the task of building the permanent bridge across this river. The work was halted for over three weeks because of two lions. Twenty-eight coolies, one European, and countless Africans lost their lives to these man-eaters. The Indians tried in vain to murder Patterson, suspecting he was somehow responsible for the man-eaters, and later 800 of them mutinied and boarded a goods train bound for Mombasa. With only a skeleton crew, Patterson stayed up every night for several weeks until the lions finally had the bad sense to stalk him and meet their timely end. To his surprise, both animals were maneless—hardly the MGM variety we suspect all man-eaters to resemble. The two animals are now on display in the Field Museum in Chicago. Patterson's only son, Brian Patterson, once showed me the original copy of the epic poem presented to his father by a certain Roshan on behalf of all the other Indians. It ends:

But for the sake of our lives, Patterson Sahib took all this trouble, risking his own life in the forest. . . . Patterson Sahib has left me, and I shall miss him as long as I live, and now,
Roshan must roam about in Africa, sad and regretful.

The Tsavo Bridge, though, is hardly spectacular. The Germans blew up Patterson's at the beginning of the First World War, and this new one is of that dull but serviceable design characterizing so much of the colonial architecture in Kenya. "That's where the original bridge was. You can just make out a pylon," Alan points out. I see nothing but a troop of baboons shambling along the bank.

We reached Voi shortly before sunset. "That's what we need," Alan says. Engine No. 5506 has caught his eye. It is an old coal-burning locomotive that has been left here to die. "Let's restore it to what it was in 1945. It'll be perfect."

Our minds are racing now. Night has fallen. All the lights blaze through the carriages hurtling through the night for Mombasa. Mackinnon Road, Taru, Samburu, Maji ya Chumvi are merely flashing glimpses of a water tank and a waving stationmaster. "It's too short," everyone is telling me. "We could stay on the train for a week and never be bored."

"The next time the Iron Snake rolls, it should start from Lake Victoria," I suggest to Geoff.

"And then another could begin from Thomson's Falls."

"Perfect, but don't forget Lake Magadi and the Nguruman."

"And we can always make a stop at Nakuru to see the birds at Lake Baringo and Hannington."

"We'll carry horses with us in a railroad horse box, and every morning we'll be able to ride through the bush."

"Maybe a Toyota or two carried on a flatbed car won't be such a bad idea either."

Plans all become magic as our glowing palace plummets toward the Indian Ocean, the engine's whistle sounding like an old mammoth's bellow. By now we all would agree with Winston Churchill, who traveled this same track in 1907 and called it "one of the most romantic and most wonderful railways in the world," and with Theodore Roosevelt, who eight years later found it to be "a railroad through the Pleistocene . . . the most interesting railway journey in the world." Tonight we know the adventure has been unimpaired over seventy years.

Nearly fifteen years have passed since I wrote this account of that epic train journey. While such a private train journey can still be arranged at considerable cost through Abercrombie and Kent, the joy of such railway travel can still be experienced on the regular evening run.

I'm still lulled by the sounds of those words: "the Iron Snake"; and I can still recall a blast of heat upon arriving at the sea in Mombasa the next morning. For nearly two days we had all felt like pashas. Some went home deluded into thinking Africa was filled with luxuries undreamed of anywhere else in the world.

Ever since, I've considered a few ironies: It is told that Mbatian, chief of the Masai, had a dream in the 1870s, long before he had ever encountered a white man. The dream spelled out that an iron snake would one day divide his land. It must have been heresy for a nineteenth-century Masai to conceive of such a threat—they being the most feared and ruthless tribe in East Africa. For years afterward, the dream haunted Mbatian. Sure enough, in 1896 the first steel rail was belted to the earth. By 1901 the tracks had reached the lake, and by 1909 the Masai had been moved off their lands, divided and effectively destroyed as a fighting nation by the settlers brought to East Africa by the Iron Snake.

Ironies abound. Today, in the succeeding nanosecond of the earth's history since I traveled the Iron Snake, most of the elephants and all the rhino we took for granted have been exterminated by poachers. The great herds of Tsavo can only be restored to the balance of fifteen years ago by a massive human exertion of honesty and bravery. Most wildlife leaders feel that more than fifteen years will be needed.

Yet, the Nairobi–Mombasa line should still be traveled. It remains the absolute African extravaganza: open to wind and smell, the haphazardness of history, the rot of rain, the relentlessness of drought, the regret of a collective human conscience. On a train in Africa one can throw away the schedule and learn a continent's patience. On this train, believe it or not, I was not the only one to learn my insolent place in history.

A D V I S O R Y

Traveling by Train

Safari operator Abercrombie and Kent can organize a trip similar to the one described above. In general, however, train travel in Africa is only for the stout-hearted. Above all, it requires a sense of humor.

• The cleanest and most pleasant regularly scheduled trip is the Kenya Railway's overnight train from Nairobi to Mombasa, though the quality of the service is unpredictable. For around $30 per person (first class), you'll get a taste of old-style train travel, complete with dinner served on china and linen in the dining car. Any tour operator can book this trip for you. Order your bedding in advance, and after dinner you'll be rocked to sleep in your bunk as the rumbling train tunnels through the darkness.

The railway follows a romantic route: You will be on the same railbed that carried Winston Churchill on *My African Journey*, Teddy Roosevelt heading toward *African Game Trails*, and you will pass very close to where Major Patterson dispatched the famed *Maneaters of Tsavo*. Be sure to take a copy of Charles Miller's *The Lunatic Express* for history and entertainment.

Flying is faster, but the night train is still the best way to get from Nairobi to the coast, if only for the sense of history it imparts. Back in the colonial nineteenth century, when the British government ordered a 1000-kilometer railroad to be constructed across the African wilderness from the coast of Kenya to the remote shores of Lake Victoria, it was quickly dubbed "the Lunatic Line" by the many who believed it was an impossible dream. But in August 1896, the track was begun in Mombasa, and after much turmoil, expense, disease, and delay, it reached Lake Victoria in 1901. It quickly became and remains a vital artery for trade, agriculture, and passengers in Kenya. A fitting beginning to your trip would be a visit to the Railway Museum in Nairobi for a dose of history and a glimpse at the polished relics of the railroad's past.

Today, visitors find Kenya Railway's Mombasa Line to be essentially a decompression chamber from the cool, near-alpine weather up-country to the sultriness of the seaside. You wake up in Mombasa, where you should head directly to the terrace of the old Castle Hotel for breakfast.

• In Zimbabwe, the best train trip is also an overnight train, from Bulawayo to Victoria Falls, arriving at the grand Victoria Falls Hotel in time for breakfast. The old-world train, with its varnished wood, lounge, and library, recalls the style of the 1930s. You can book a "steam safari" through a travel agent or contact Rail Safaris, Zambia House, Union Avenue, P.O. Box 4070, Harare, Zimbabwe; tel. 263-4 736056 in Harare, or 263-30673 in Bulawayo.

• Tanzania's railway, from Dar es Salaam to Kigoma, is for the highly adventuresome only. There is no telling what time it will leave and how many days the trip will take. Though it's dusty and primitive, it's one way to experience what Africa is really like. You won't see any non-Africans here aside from an occasional backpacker, and you'll be just as likely to rub shoulders with chickens and goats. Stout-hearted souls can contact the Tanzania Railway Corporation (Sokoine Drive, P.O. Box 486, Dar es Salaam, Tanzania, tel. 255-51-26241; telex 41308).

Victoria Falls, Zimbabwe

5

THE
ROMANTIC
HOTELS
OF AFRICA

THE MOST ROMANTIC OF ALL HOTELS IS

no more. Owned by Toni Nutti, an Italian frontierswoman, it could accommodate at one time fewer than ten guests. This remote lodge was indeed her home, suffocating under bougainvillaea, surrounded by the rapids of the Kagera River, with views of the plains of Tanzania on one side and a Uganda escarpment on the other.

Mrs. Nutti was supposed to pay taxes to Uganda, but since she had little time for authority, she rarely answered her mail and saw off anyone wearing a uniform. Her link with the outside world was a manual cable car, cranked by a seven-foot-tall Watusi warrior. Sometimes she tuned into the BBC, but on most evenings she and her guests preferred listening to the gruntings of the pet hippos in the river pools outside the drawing room, and watching, through the porch screens, the silhouettes of butterflies, many of them still not recorded by lepidopterists. Toni had once loved a distinguished British game warden and often in the early dark of Africa, with the yip of hyenas emerging as melody to the chorus of waters, she would speak of him as though neither one belonged to this world. Indeed, this island was a no-man's land, and since it was ruled with such reverence for nature, one easily forgot the time, the passport, even thoughts of home.

There have been times since then when, recalling that comfortably forlorn home, the charging waters that fenced it from banality, and its charming seigneure, I became irritable with sentimentality and dismissed the memory as a mere fillip of history. "Romance is irrelevant," I might have said to myself, overcome by a recurring suspicion that there is a grander scheme for memory. "What, after all, is a place like that good for?"

Quite a lot, I now believe.

When I travel, I often pack a copy of *Other Men's Flowers*, an anthology of poetry compiled by Field Marshall Earl Wavell. In his introduction, which I have read in places like the Des Moines Holiday Inn, he writes, "The aim of the lyrical poet, as of the stage manager, is to create glamour and illusion that will take our minds from the common circumstances of everyday life and fix them on the world as it ought to be. . . ."

Toni Nutti's river island was, for a time, what the world ought to be. Three long-ago days there are still an antidote to what I despairingly call the "real world." Just as Lord Wavell recited his beloved poems "to forget the dreariness of war," so too have I exploited my brief memory of a Xanadu.

Africa is for me the most romantic of the earth's surfaces, perhaps because I can never forget it was where man was born. On savannah, by river, at swamp's edge, in slum, or simple village, I am convinced I am watching life still in rehearsal. Even to be an understudy on such a stage of evolution chills me with promise I have found nowhere else.

Ever since Toni Nutti died in the Ugandan revolution, I have tried to find other windows to Africa equal to hers. My search has acquainted me with wonderful hotels and lodges, some of them far more luxurious than hotels in Europe or America. But chocolates on the bed pillows at night do not make for romance. So I looked beyond frills for incorruptible qualities—for locations that arouse an atavistic chill, for spots that disclose heart, lung, and tissue of Africa. On this search I found a hotel near a waterfall, a river, a swamp, a plain, a settlement, and the African sea. And each hotel has its own set of peculiar idiosyncrasies.

That is certainly true with the Victoria Falls Hotel. Recently painted an excruciating lime green, it appears to be making fun of its own colonial past. I was at first appalled at its bizarre mod look, for I had known this Zimbabwe landmark twenty years before,

when any color other than white would have been unthinkable. On returning this time, I was filled with memories of heavy deck chairs where district officers, enjoying their first leave in years, luxuriated, occasionally pulling a Meerschaum pipe out from their white knee socks, and talking "elephant control" with sad wives wearing fashions a decade out of date. Alan Moorehead loved this hotel, too. I can remember in *No Room in the Ark* his account of waking late at night and seeing beyond the mosquito netting the shadow of a baboon, peering at him through the window.

Built in 1904, the hotel was sited so that visitors had a view, not of the falls, but of that other wonder—man's ingenuity—a metal suspension bridge spanning the gorge and representing a cog in Cecil Rhodes' dream of a Cape to Cairo railroad. During the intervening years the hotel has been touched very considerably by the African railroad system, and even now when a lonely whistle blows, it means the overnight from Bulawayo has just arrived beyond the gate of the hotel.

Independence and revolution, rifle fire across the gorge, an unfortunate kidnapping of tourists by rebels have all affected the seasonal fortunes of this once grand hotel. But today, with President Mugabe now the peacemaker, overseas visitors are returning to Zimbabwe. The current manager told me he had, in fact, "just let one hundred thirty-nine of my one hundred thirty-seven rooms!"

This gentleman, no student of the colonial past, is delighted with his color sense, and believes that it is one cause of the hotel's success. In addition to his creation of the electric exterior, he has transformed the dining room into a pink wedding cake; the hallways he has shrouded in varying shades of Wedgwood green. In the evenings on the terrace where once the orchestra played "The Merry Widow Waltz," today a Jamaican marimba band entertains buxom Shona ladies under a string of lightbulbs, each one a different color.

Still, there is an allure here no color will ever change. One glimpses it in the inner courtyard, shaded by mango trees; in the reflecting pools, filled with bream and goldfish, descendants of fish born here when this land was known as Southern Rhodesia; at the "swimming bath"; on the tennis courts. False mahogany trees on the terrace present a canopy to chairs laid out meticulously as if they were on the promenade deck of the *Queen Mary*. And the staff of 300, some still dressed in sashes, honor the hush of long corridors decorated with Thomas Baines prints, now faded.

The falls are the source of the hotel's romance. For most of its 1500 miles the Zambezi appears a tired, mature river given to still pools and muddy banks, but here it suffers momentary insanity. Breaking over a bedrock chasm, it dumps 500 million liters of water a minute (and sometimes an injudicious hippo) into boiling pools 350 feet below. So great is the river's recklessness that the spray leaps 1500 feet into the air. *Mosi ya tunya*—"the smoke that thunders"—was what local tribes called it when David Livingstone claimed it in 1855 for Britain. He thought he was doing it a favor by replacing this alluring name with that of a monarch who was never to set foot in Africa. Today Queen Victoria is remembered in another way: In the hotel bar, a cocktail has been created in her honor.

The falls are hardly changed since Livingstone's day. Gravel footpaths lead from one vantage point to the next, and the only safety fencing consists of impromptu thorns. Since the path system is so extensive, rarely does one encounter hordes, as one might on any other continent. The best time to see the falls is at dawn, when only baboons and bushbuck use these paths. The roar of water, the rising mist, this vertigo landscape prepare one for a philosophical breakfast at the hotel. But delay it ten minutes by returning via the railroad station to meet the morning train, still pulled by a coal-fired steam engine. Here, do as I did: Watch the cool greetings and farewells of this fiery continent and see the faces of a new Africa, peering out of bundles on their mothers' backs.

Botswana's Chobe Game Lodge, fifty miles from the falls, is not my choice for one of Africa's romantic hotels merely because Richard Burton and Elizabeth Taylor were remarried here. There

is a better reason: the Chobe River—aortic, sensual, seminal. Joseph Conrad wrote of another such artery: "What greatness has not floated on the ebb of that river into the mystery of an unknown earth. . . . The dreams of men . . . the germs of empire."

The Chobe, rising in Angola, flowing sometimes east, sometimes west, is Conrad's river. My notes read: "A storm is being mounted from across the frontier in the Caprivi Strip. The wind blows against the river's current, chuffing the trees. The fish eagle stops calling. Cormorants, looking like gargoyles, retract their wings, anticipating even stronger winds. Clouds, once mere brushstrokes, bundle, whirl, and circle our patch of riverbank. Warthogs flee from the wind—a large family all with their tails straight up. Thunder booms, circling for a kill. Leaves droop, reeds flatten. One drop falls, and in no time the storm is upon us with such fury that rainwater is propelled seven feet into the air out of the bottoms of gutters. Conversations cease. Whether rain or hail—when it hits the roof it sounds like automatic gunfire. This storm, flashing, booming, gushing, won't permit us to consider any other notion."

The Chobe Game Reserve is a brilliantly kept secret; it possesses many of the highly touted attributes of more famous parks, but here crowds are absent. As one travels south from the river, the vegetation thins, tall canopies of *Acacia nigrensis* by the river giving way to the shadeless mopane trees, which are harbingers of the Kalahari Desert. Elephants, leaving catapulted trees in their path, silently commute, like suburbanites, between the river and this bushland. In the dry season, the game—indigenous antelopes like tsessebe, puku, and lechwe, wildebeest, and zebra—is within a few feet of the hotel. Hardly a night passes without baboons making a nuisance of themselves on the terrace. And in the river, at cocktail hour, battle-scarred hippos lunge and yawn, preparing for nighttime forays on the hotel lawn.

By rights, the lodge—half adobe, half Moorish—should appear a non sequitur in the middle of Africa. But it works. There are few walls in the public rooms, so the wind can visit the bar and the dining room, rattling fine African masks set in alcoves and billowing the doilies that cover the midday smörgåsbord. In the bedrooms the ceilings are vaulted and the lamps made of tooled calabashes. There are four suites, each with its private swimming pool, overlooking (as does every room at Chobe) Conrad's river.

The days here are timed to animals—dawn awakenings to watch mongooses from a Land Rover, after-breakfast trolling for tiger fish, evening cocktails on the river launch, observed by crocodiles and sacred ibis. Wildlife becomes an obsession and only the street-hardened can resist a temptation to bring field glasses to lunch on the verandah, just in case a coucal perched nearby calls.

Flying south, the view from the plane's window is at first of desolation, not romance. "Here in Botswana," says Paul Rawson, pilot and co-owner of Xaxaba Camp, our destination, "we are great believers in the Flat Earth Society." Beneath us: not a ripple resembling a hill, not a road. Game trails, feeding into dry wa-terholes, might be an electron micrograph image of brain neurons linked to each other by filaments of dendrites. Gray here, khaki there. A lone tree is a celebration.

Suddenly, beneath us there appears a sharp demarcation: The waters of the Okavango Delta have begun. Now we might as well be flying over a golf course with occasional sand traps, lots of water hazards, and very slim fairways (which on closer investigation become stands of papyrus). In all these almost 7000 square miles of land-locked delta, there are but three minute hills to serve as landmarks for a pilot. Paul Rawson, however, knows this wilderness so well that he is happy to turn the Cessna in a full circle to point out what most eyes cannot see. He tells of the recently rediscovered tribe of river Bushmen who once inhabited these waterways. Today only one, Xaxanam (the "x's" are pronounced as clicks), survives, on an island with one stump called Xigere. Paul mentions the rain tree beneath us—a tree that, thanks to the spittlebug, can create a midday shower for those camped in its shade. He speaks of islands in the Delta, seen by man only from the air. He quotes a friend, saying, "Sea of land, land of water," and then shakes his

head in wonderment, still moved by the sight of the great natural phenomenon that has been his family home for the last three years.

The Okavango River rises in the highlands of Angola a few hundred miles from the Atlantic, and spends its career searching for the Indian Ocean. It never succeeds. Instead, it settles on evaporating across this mantle of sand, the southernmost extension of Africa's Great Rift. Every year the waters rise in the Delta, paradoxically during the dry season, six months after they were produced by the Angolan floods. Every year, too, islands are formed in the Okavango, mostly by termites and birds. The termites create mounds and the birds deposit seeds in the mounds. As a result, almost every tree in the Okavango bears either fruit or nuts. This swamp, not Babylon, is my choice for the site of the Garden of Eden.

Penny and Paul Rawson have bet their life savings on the hunch that others will find this aquatic cornucopia bewitching. Access is exclusively by light aircraft, and only eighteen guests can share the island with them at any one time. Accommodations are huts of split papyrus and thatch, each with attached dressing room, bath, and human-free view of the island. The Rawsons are very sensible people, as pilots must be, but occasionally they admit to whimsy, like the huge mirror they installed behind the bar, to show their beloved Delta backwards.

Like them, one becomes obsessed with this watery world and the serendipity of life it celebrates. At sunset each day, one must be on the water, preferably in a makoro canoe, poled by Fish, the chief designate of the Batawana tribe. The sky becomes a sea of different ideas—spun cotton to the west, a cork of rain to the north, dark fudge to the south. A collared dove sounds his six notes. A squacco heron leaves a trail of muddled water before he reaches flight speed. A pied kingfisher, with full flaps, circles a dream of dinner. A lilytrotter coasts through the reeds, its outstretched legs a bunch of asparagus. Spurwing geese. Pygmy geese. Snake eagles. Around Xaxaba there are some 308 different species of birds, living on 1000 different plants, off 200 species of tree. And while you observe, your bottom stays dry, on the hardwood hull beneath the surface of the water, with Fish silently propelling you against the mysterious currents of indefinable channels.

The romance of the Delta is created by its quirky abundance. The desert lies a half-hour flight away, still inhabited by Bushmen who will spend the day stockpiling enough water to fill one ostrich egg. Why is it that here the water laps at one's feet, threatening to put out the evening campfire?

Two thousand miles to the north, there is another kind of profligacy. The wildebeest migration across the Serengeti/Masai Mara ecosystem is the sort of waste that only nature can afford. Last year some 1.6 million animals covered nearly 2000 miles, leaving a near-continuous trail of dead along the way. It didn't matter. The herd benefited, and for anyone lucky to witness this ceremony of survival it was the consummate lesson in natural selection.

In the Masai Mara there are many tented camps. My favorites are Kichwa Tembo, Cottar's Camp, and Little Governor's Camp.

Canvas was made for Africa. It allows the sleeper to be awakened by noises too subtle to be heard in a permanent structure. It seems to tremble to a lion's roar, and sometimes, if one is very lucky (in adventure), as I have been, it may snap and spring should a hippo choose to graze between the guy ropes. There were times when all I ever thought a foreigner could sensibly own in Africa was just that—a tent. This continent simply does not tolerate more extensive claims of tenure. And a tent reveals the heart of the land: Pitch your home by this water hole and you own the water hole—until an elephant disputes your claim, or the rains fail, or your food supply dwindles. A tent is a happy reminder of one's own puniness.

For many years only the Ernest Hemingways and Robert Ruarks—the hunters—understood this verity. The camera bugs stayed in hardrock lodges with curtains drawn. But beginning in 1965 there was a boom in this new type of permanent installation. Kichwa Tembo was erected about ten years later, with greater

luxuries than most of the others. Basically, this is a hotel: The tents are numbered, the bathrooms attached, the showers dependable. The dining room used to be a tent; now it is a permanent structure. In the kitchen there is one reminder of the old camping days: The cook still does his baking in a tin trunk set in coals in the fashion of Kipkoski, Ruark's cook of several decades past.

The romance of this country derives from grass. Driving through the wind-blown savannah at dusk one can spot nearly every link in the food chain. European storks, just arrived from the chimney pots of Istanbul, are having a feast on soldier ants emerging out of the ground between grass stems. A martial eagle annihilates one such stork too distracted by the feast, while a herd of elephants graze a few feet away, encouraging more soldier ants to take wing. Exactly 100 yards away a cheetah sits on an anthill and waits for a topi (an antelope) sampling new grass to make one false move. A little over two miles beyond, an old lion tries not to notice that his nine cubs are alternately pulling his tail, suckling his nonexistent teats, and tugging at his mane. Just occasionally, perhaps recalling he is king of the jungle, he curls his lips, still blood-stained from a young gazelle who was this morning too obsessed by new grass to look up in time.

One is comforted in daylight by such neat connections. But at night Africa seems only to pose problems. Why does the bush baby cry out from the river? Is that a leopard coughing? Are the Masai tribesmen, armed with only spears, scared of the dark? What is the lion saying?

Admittedly, the fire is reassuring. It transforms this vast land into a circle of fluttering amber, forty feet around. But then just as one becomes comfortable with a canvas chair and a Tusker beer, there, out of the blackness, thirty-four eyes—count them—watch you. Must be Thomson gazelles. Who then is the watcher, who the watched?

Peponi's Hotel, only 500 miles away, might as well be in a different land. Located near Shella, a village on an island just off the Kenya coast, it is the final resolution of a safari. To the southwest, just out of sight, lie eight miles of soft sand beach that locals will call crowded if ten people are visible in all its length. To the northwest towers a great sand dune where the bones of victims of a battle fought 175 years ago are still exposed after a wind. And two miles due north from here lies Lamu, a small Arab town still ignorant of cars and bicycles. There the streets, just wide enough to allow two fully laden donkeys to pass, are enclosed by coral townhouses, some four stories tall. There a man's wives, draped in black formless *buibuis*, their hands painted with henna, their mouths purple from chewing betel nut, sometimes can be heard singing behind shuttered windows. There in the evenings old *nakhodas* (sea captains) converge on the wide plaza by the harbor, sit on the cannons facing the sea, and talk of storms.

By peering through one teakwood door here at Peponi's one faces this Swahili world. By opening the other, one hears the tide bursting upon a coral reef and feels the first flush of the Kazkazi, the northeast trades. Peponi's commands a headland between the world of traditional peoples and the lie of a lonely sea.

Wera Korshen, a Danish widow who has run Peponi's ever since her husband sold his up-country farm, would have one believe hers is no different from any hotel. But there is a twinkle in Wera's eyes when she painstakingly dismisses the little niceties—the rooms designed to amplify the call of the muezzin urging the faithful to prayer, the black floors that gleam at all hours, the freshly squeezed lime juice always on the bar, the jasmine petals scattered on the bed pillows at night, the private verandahs designed to allow one to observe the great ocean-going dhows beating into the harbor in the last hours of their 2000 years of history.

And on an evening of the full moon, Wera will be the first to invite you aboard her *jihazi*, an open dhow, for a sail into the harbor of Lamu and beyond. The fresh mangrove oysters will be served in their shells, the lobsters will be roasted over a brazier off the stern, and the sea will catch the moon's glare, casting it back as if each wave were the scale of a fish, as you head toward Africa and home.

On a night such as this, one thinks perhaps of the question Isak Dinesen, author of that brillant *Out of Africa*, once asked: "If I know a song of Africa . . . of the giraffe, and the African new moon lying on her back . . . does Africa know a song of me? Would the air over the plain quiver with a colour that I had had on, or the children invent a game in which my name was, or the full moon throw a shadow over the gravel of the drive that was like me, or would the eagles of Ngong look out for me?"

Perhaps it is because we know the contemptuous answer to her question that we return to Africa time and again. Such is romance.

A D V I S O R Y
If You Want Romance

Inexpensive ($) . . . . . . $30–$70
Moderate ($$) . . . . $70–$150
Expensive ($$$) . . . . . $150–$300
Very expensive ($$$$) $300 and up

The one carrier that connects all five romantic hotels with North America and Europe is British Airways. To reach Victoria Falls, fly first to Harare, Zimbabwe, and onward via Zimbabwe Air. Reservations can be made by writing: **Victoria Falls Hotel**, P.O. Box 10, Victoria Falls, Zimbabwe (tel. 263-13-203/4/5; telex 3324). Rates: $$. I recommend asking for the Lobengula Suite if one wishes to face the courtyard, or the Batoka Suite for the best view of the gorge. Best time: year round.

Transport is available in Victoria Falls for the short drive to Chobe. Reservations: **Chobe Game Lodge (Pty) Limited**, P.O.

Box 782597, Sandton 2146, South Africa (tel. 27-331 3934/5; telex 8-6129 SA). Some suites have private swimming pools. Rates: $$$. Suite 210 (the site of the Burton honeymoon) is my favorite. Try to avoid rooms numbered under 100, for they tend to be noisy. The best time for game-viewing is June through October, although in October the weather tends to be steamy. While it may rain in December, and the game may be slightly dispersed, there probably is no more beautiful time, with great storm clouds building through the open sky each afternoon.

The Rawsons will fly you from Chobe to Xaxaba. Reservations: **Xaxaba Camp**, P.O. Box 147, Maun, Botswana (no phone; telex 2482 BD). Rates: $$. I liked all the 9 huts.

The journey onward to Kenya can be negotiated via Johannesburg or Harare. On British Airways the flight will last about four hours. To reach **Kichwa Tembo** from Nairobi, there is a daily Sunbird DC-3 flight, popularly known as the "Vomit Comet." Reservations: **Signet Hotels**, P.O. Box 59749, Nairobi, Kenya (tel. 254-2-334955; telex 22853 Kentours). Rates: $$$. Best time: any month with the exception of April, May, and the first half of June—the time of the long rains. I recommend tents numbered 16 and 17, the honeymoon suite, "VK," and 21 through 25.

To travel to Peponi's, one must first return to Nairobi. Once a week there is a direct but not very dependable flight to Manda Island, adjacent to Lamu. Otherwise, fly on the daily Air Kenya flight to Malindi, where one can catch a twice daily and quite predictable flight to Manda. From here the hotel will meet you in their kerosene-powered launch, which takes about half an hour to reach the hotel. Reservations: **Peponi Hotel**, P.O. Box 24, Lamu, Kenya (tel. 29; telex Peponi Lamu). Rates: $$$. Best time: The hotel is closed in May and June. Christmas reservations, as with all the other romantic hotels, are usually booked a year in advance. I recommend January through the end of March as the most dependable weather period. For a room with privacy and the best views, I recommend 16, 16A, 18 through 20, and what Wera calls the "top room."

To arrange all the above with one phone call, contact **Abercrombie and Kent International Inc.**, 1000 Oak Brook Road, Oak Brook, IL 60521 (tel. 312-887-7766 or 800-323-7308).

On the West Coast: **Bryan International Travel Inc.**, 421 Powell Street, Suite 210, San Francisco, CA 94102 (tel. 415-9876-0967).

In the South: **Osborne Travel**, 3379 Peach Tree Road, N.E., Atlanta, GA 30326 (tel. 404-261-1600).

In the East: **Continental American Travel Inc.**, 770 Lexington Avenue, New York, NY 10021 (tel. 212-759-8302).

A D V I S O R Y

A Special Case of Romance

For the last fifteen years, hotels in Tanzania have, for the most part, fallen on hard times. "No ice," "no soap," "no lightbulbs," often "no running water" were among the more serene of travelers' complaints.

During this period one hostelry defied local conventions, by virtue of the high standards and calm stubbornness of its management. Gibb's Farm is about 4 miles from the village of Karatu, off the potholed main road linking the gateway town of Arusha with Lake Manyara, the Ngorongoro Crater, and the Serengeti. Margaret Gibb originally felt more at home with coffee growing than with hotel management, but when commodity markets turned against her, especially after her husband's death, she started serving luncheons for road-weary tourists on their way towards the wildebeest herds.

Since then, Gibb's Farm has prospered as one of East Africa's only authentic country inns. Set in some of the loveliest gardens of East Africa, overlooking a valley planted in coffee, it is at the crossroads of travel in northern Tanzania. Most safari outfitters, upon discovering this oasis, book their clients merely for Gibb's extraordinary lunches. I recommend going farther and spending a night at this glorious place. This pause in your whirligig road journey will give you time to adjust to a glorious African quiet of crackling fires, uniformed waiters, and the distant monsoon of cicadas in the acacia trees. With hardly more than 20 beds to fill, the farmhouse becomes effectively your own home.

After dinner Margaret Kullander (she married the ranch manager, a former Olympic miler), if she is not at her other magnificent hotel in the Serengeti (Ndutu Lodge), will primly tantalize you with a story about a leopard that patrols through the coffee, or with a news bulletin about the gang of poachers bivouacked in the forest, ready to attack the hotel for its cache of petrol. While Margaret seems to have leaped from an E. M. Forster tea party, her Third World empire is cut from the pages of V. S. Naipaul.

While there is little game to be seen in the gardens, Gibb's gentle views of the slopes of Ngorongoro, the neat lushness of its landscaping, the ice-cold drinks, and shadowy walks will emerge as one of the highlights of your Tanzanian safari.

Rhino and calf, Ngorongoro Crater, Tanzania

6

AFRICA LOG:

A Family Safari

19 DECEMBER, THE NORTH ATLANTIC:

Two hours out of JFK I've begun my first nature notes for this African safari. My eighteen companions, drawn and pasty-faced from school, vineyard, office, and last-minute repacking, are sprawled in seats behind me, almost all asleep, although our 747 has just made an emergency landing in Gander. News that some rock star's girl friend in first class has been hemorrhaging uncontrollably since we reached altitude has had more of an impact on those over forty than on those still in school, innocent of our generation's primal urge to gossip.

I look at my niece, the Smithy, curled like an angora on the master's chair. Perfect insouciance: She is the one responsible, the one who teased me, one Thanksgiving before last, into believing I would be a world-class failure unless I tested myself as a family courier. "You know you promised me when I was six, you'd take me to Africa." Twirling a strand of hair around a finger and saying nothing else, she had seemed the perfect embodiment of conscience for a bachelor uncle. Now, on the blackest of sub-arctic winter nights, as Canadian orderlies remove a slightly empty rock star's girl friend, the Smithy's eyelids flutter with rapid eye movements. Her face mirrors nothing but the languor of being twenty-one. Africa might as well be Springfield, Mass. And all uncles Santa Claus. My niece is dreaming.

Thanks to her, Mr. Nice Guy's responsibilities grew. There was another niece, age four, who had precociously gotten hold of a fully illustrated version of *Born Free* and started chatting up perfect strangers with lion stories. Now a nephew, a sister, a brother and all his in-laws, a family friend, her son, his cousin, as well as my father's horse racing partner and his entire hominid brood were in attendance. (By now the group had grown too much for my father and his wife, so they chose to make other plans.)

None seemed sensitive to my predicament, that the continent they were moving in on en masse had been a *private* sanctuary for me since age sixteen. Looking through the hushed aircraft, I thought: Wasn't Africa going to be awfully small for this lot? Won't the city-dwellers be bored by the natural history? Isn't the sixty-eight-year-old going to be distressed by the dust? Won't the young one be ravaged by internal parasites like bilharzia? And the adolescents—no doubt they'll be much too raucous. Won't all these polished Americans, harmonious in their own environment, disturb the equilibrium, the symmetry, and the secret of my Africa? Worst of all, aren't they all going to become public risks in the Serengeti?

21 December, Meru Game Lodge, northern Tanzania: Thank God the sun has set; the full enormity of this undertaking has caused a slight hand tremble. I recklessly order a second Tembo beer and wonder what has possessed me to assume such responsibility. This morning the nineteen of us, now recovered from jet lag and the effects of a curry lunch in a Nairobi back street, had been met by Abercrombie and Kent minibuses at the Norfolk Hotel. Nineteen relatives means three times nineteen pieces of luggage. It also means forgetfulness. "Has anyone seen my camera bag?" a voice wails, the innuendo being that the Nikons were nicked by a busboy. For American travelers in the Third World, it seems suspicion comes first, then the revelation of one's own forgetfulness. I think of Teddy Roosevelt, who in 1909 drank a pink gin without ice on the terrace of this same hotel while waiting for his 500 safari porters to gather their sixty-pound loads and give the signal to depart. He, at least, only had his son Kermit to consider.

The only one unimpressed by the incongruity of her eighteen

kinsmen driving past Kilimanjaro is the four-year-old, kitted out in a khaki skirt, khaki shirt, and a white hat and looking like Tilly in *The Flame Trees of Thika*. Throughout the drive south from Nairobi, the torturous wait in the Tanzanian customs hut at Namanga, and along the potholed road past Arusha, she had been exemplary.

But I can see our company has at last begun to afflict her. In the half-light, the view from the verandah of this hotel is of a too green lawn, set with deck chairs, separated by a ditch from the musky bush where flamingoes wade, egrets nest, waterbuck graze, warthogs root. As cousins contemplate the meaning of paradise, my sister sins against her four-year-old's nature by informing her that it is now time for bed. This littlest of all imperialists looks her mum straight in the eyes: "I'm going to run away from you, and you're never going to see me again." My noisy family hushes. Even my sister seems floored, as her Cabbage Patch feminist tightens the belt of her dressing gown, picks up the half-empty Coke bottle, and sets off into the night. In her first few steps, her freedom seems assured, but then shadows deepen. Her quick step falters and, as she tests Africa's penumbra at the edge of the verandah's light, the lion roars. It is, in truth, a caged, probably toothless lion in the Arusha zoo, but it does the trick. The runaway leaps into her mother's arms.

24 December, the Ngorongoro Crater: Three days is all it takes for each newcomer to Africa to stop talking about home. On the first day, one intoned menacing refrains about his stepfather, dead for ten years, whenever our guide, Rick Mathews, paused to explain lion behavior. Others merely grew mute, retiring into private whimsies. I had never before stopped to consider how shockingly unfamiliar Africa must be to most Americans. The ground hornbill appears to have stepped out of the Pleistocene; and the only way to appreciate fully the symmetry of, say, a Thomson gazelle is to understand just how readily it can be returned to its maker by a leopard.

Now, citified noses, ears, and eyes are beginning to reassemble the ironies of natural history into a rough and cynical order. Acacia trees are no longer confused for giraffes. And what on the first evening was identified as raw potatoes is now understood to be the smell of rotting vegetation.

Most comments about the Ngorongoro Crater have now become lavish hyperbole. This morning, when we interrupted the morning game drive for a picnic breakfast on Enkitate Hill, strung like a belt across the midriff of the caldera floor, our safari's wise-ass stopped his one-liners long enough to say, "This kind of beauty isn't supposed to happen."

Below us, the antique path of a dry river can be charted by a filigree of acacia trees. A mile away, buffaloes charge in our direction out of the shimmer of the crater lake, their backs epoxied with mud. Above them, a flume of egrets coils through the morning sky, waiting for their quixotic perches to resume grazing. Rick Mathews, stripped to the waist, stands solemnly on this treeless hill, one extended arm proffering the heel of the breakfast bread loaf. A moment later, a yellow-billed kite with laser vision dives soundlessly at this human target; in a flash before striking, it extends its talons, rakes Rick's hand, retrieves breakfast, and hauls back into the blue. Above the hollow of its near soundless flight comes a new distraction—distant gongs and pings of Masai cattle bells. Somewhere on another rise, a naked six-year-old must be throwing pebbles at his father's principal investment to keep it from stampeding into this oasis land at the foot of the crater, restricted by law to "God's cattle." And directly above us, in a sky innocent of clouds, a lappet-faced vulture swirls, waiting for the long-distance smell of blood.

Yesterday, everyone might have chimed in with remarks. Today, most are struck dumb. Only the cynic dares talk. "Isn't nature a son-of-a-bitch?"

Christmas Day: Because nineteen people exceed the legal limits of many Tanzania campsites, our total party has been split in two; while we come to grips with the walled intimacy of the

Crater, the others have been enjoying the great sweeps of the Serengeti. Today we rotate; the Serengeti group (known by us as the "B Team") will overlap long enough here for a joint Christmas lunch, and then we transfer onto the great plains after a drive of four hours.

In another place and age I might have stayed awake on Christmas Eve to hear the sound of Santa's reindeer slipping on shingles; last night I was awakened to lions after a kill. Their roaring was more than MGM; it seemed to have been created by giant bellows; a weak grunt built to tent-flapping thunder. I heard family and friends in nearby tents stirring, whispering, the cooing of a mother against the querulous alarm of a child. For me the lion may as well have been celebrating the Latin Mass, a savage priest serving up his own responses. (Years ago, my wa-Kamba gunbearer assured me that the lion is always asking, "Whose land is this? Whose land is this?" And so on, only to reply, "My land," (fading) "my land," (faded) "my land . . .") Tonight, once the lion is done, the rest of the bush slowly resumes the business of the night. A tree hyrax—a rodent the size of a marmot, living in the fig tree overhead—editorializes just before dawn with a crude belch.

In the dawn overcast, the plains are replete with killers; a pride of four lions, a mile from camp, is identified as last night's celebrants. They do not even open their eyes when we park a few feet away. Their stomachs are bloated, a clue not lost on the zebra placidly grazing fifty feet downwind. A lion's life is not distinguished by subtlety.

There will be no church this Christmas. For most of my family, lapsed or with other alibis, such a loss will not be disturbing. I, however, have been considering, until the first sign of rain, the solemnity of this natural cathedral and the fair omen it embodies. Most of all, I am overjoyed that the Crater is beyond the realm of wreaths, carols, pressure to give, and the urge to get, swap, enjoin, and enjoy. Today nature is serving up this atavistic Christmas without man's legerdemain; the ionized air and the clear view of several simultaneous weather systems evoke an out-of-body spirituality, the floating narcosis of a great choir. Bat-eared foxes raise their heads, half quizzical, half wise, and I pray no one will utter a word: I am hearing the organ of the quintessential Sacre Coeur.

When the "B Team" arrives at camp just after noon in a brief interval of rain and cold, I can see that, for the most part, they too sense the "rightness" of Africa at Christmas. "Did you hear what happened to Pammy?" everyone burbles. Apparently, a few days before, my sister-in-law had ambled on foot up a kopje (an outcropping of rock) displacing a lioness, who bolted out of her way in a flash of feline muscle and sinew. But "Lionbait" (Pammy) is more considered. "The Serengeti—all that death and birth and endless grass—it's about as spiritual a place as I've ever been. If I were dying of some incurable disease, it's where I'd want to go, I guess. It's infinity . . ."

Even the four-year-old at Christmas lunch is inclined to a little philosophy. "Why do people kill rhinoceroses?" she asks as she opens her party favor. At two giant tables under a spanking new green mess tent, we have been joined by the only others camped in the crater, the world's authority on jackals and her lover, a safari operator. It had seemed perverse to have allowed them to have a Christmas meal without us.

And now the tables are filled to capacity, with some of us sitting on packing cases. The staff have been busy all morning, roasting three turkeys over an open fire, baking mince pies, and chafing five other dishes of fresh vegetables, brought from Nairobi. The kerosene refrigerators have been filled to capacity with most of a case of Moët et Chandon and no one—not even my brother, a student of Alice Waters of Chez Panisse—can sidestep hyperbole. Jonathan Kenworthy, the British sculptor and "old Africa hand," quick to find fault with most safaris, nods conspiratorially to approve. Our guest, the Danish safari operator, is so moved by the warmth of a dozen slightly inebriated new best friends that he discovers a bottle of chilled aquavit in his Land Rover. Emboldened by our warm response to his charity, he returns to his Land Rover,

this time to locate a box of his favorite cigars. Now when he returns the mood of bonhomie might have become strained. When he wets the end of his projectile and then blows expensive Canary Island smoke rings through the mess tent, five teenagers gag in unison.

Such may be the tone of family Christmases in most parts, but not what followed. Our heads spinning with fellowship and the mixture of strong drink, we drive up the wall of the Crater, head out onto the Masai Plains—the greenest, the lushest grazing I have seen this side of Montana's Big Hole—and then we descend onto the Serengeti, thunderheads boiling on the slopes behind us. Cloaked herdsmen, seemingly at one with those shepherds who once tended flocks beside the Sea of Galilee, watch us wimps of the twentieth century with thin interest. Beside them graze herds of Thomson and Grant's gazelle, wildebeest, and zebra; as the light fails, these, particularly the wildebeest, increase exponentially, so that hardly a corner of any horizon is not moving with the rhythm of little and plenty. Had we remained at home in America, Christmas evening might have been deflation after the excesses of this day. Here, as dusk gathers and the potholed track leading to camp flutters with roosting nightjars, Christmas is still to come.

27 December, camp near Lake Lagarja, the Serengeti Plains: It makes no difference to know that the Serengeti is about the size of Connecticut, for here on the plains there are no fences and the sweep of the land is so continuous it seems it must end only at the sea. Even horizons are arbitrary. At noon the land rises without a break, arguing in its own way that it belongs to the sky. And indeed in late afternoons when tumbling clouds from Ngorongoro race westward, the grasslands spin through the spectrum of blues and purples, shadowing the storm.

The Serengeti is a stunning anomaly of our times. During an era when wildlife has been threatened everywhere, here wildebeest and zebra numbers have actually increased. In 1962 the Serengeti migration was thought to comprise one quarter of a million head of wildebeest. Today, there are 1.4 million on the march—all because veterinarians eliminated rinderpest among Masai cattle in the early 1960s and unwittingly allowed wild bovids to multiply, thus restoring these plains to their mid-nineteenth-century profligacy. And in spite of uncontained poaching, a ten-year respite in tourist revenues, and the concurrent erosion in the park's administrative infrastructure, I am overcome today (as I remember being in 1961) with the notion that here, of all places, Nature is a spendthrift.

Peter Jones, in charge of our Serengeti camp, is a handsome, cowlicked stone-napper. I didn't know what "stone-napper" meant until this morning, when Peter proposed stopping the Land Cruisers underneath a grove of *Acacia xanthiflora*, thus displacing several giraffes. He then proceeded to demonstrate that we had been beaten to this spot by early man.

Along a slight drainage, the ground is peppered with stone tools once used as choppers and skinning knives. Ingenuously, Peter demonstrates how each tool had been made, perhaps 10,000 years previously, and how hunter-gatherers may have paused here to butcher—who knows?—the ancestor of that wildebeest heavy with young we just spotted on the edge of the herd. Peter's soft words and the authority he brings, as one of the earth's few stone toolmakers, are not lost on the others. The teenagers, particularly the one who originally resisted going to Africa in favor of surfing Stateside, now take up the hunt with fervor (I pray Africa may wallop him as it once did me). The other teenager, the one we call "Half Man, Half Biscuit," sprints along the drainage, filling his pocket with questions.

At half past two we reach the Moru Kopjes, a destination whose lilting name makes me squint my eyes in anticipation wherever I am. Kopjes, sometimes known as *inselbergs*, are no more than rocky outcroppings. On roadless plains in the Serengeti, they become bearings, as well as the dynamic synthesis of our dim understanding of how a great system of nature works. "Imagine these plains a sea," Peter had explained at dinner last night. "Kopjes are moun-

taintops of Precambrian stone from the earth's mantle. Buried by miles and miles of volcanic ash, they peer out as if they are islands in a sea of grass . . ."

We middle-aged types have all been told never to expect to change the nature of others, yet today I bet a few of these kids, strangers to Africa until last week, are discovering in themselves a flame never before set or extinguished. Peter leads the way into a cave. On a wall crenellated by erosion, water seepage, and maybe campfire smoke, long-ago hunters run after an exquisitely rendered giraffe. Overlying these are the designs of Masai shields, the doodling of not-so-long-ago poachers. The floor on which we stand once was a bed for humans who had never known metal or fabrics and could not understand the possibilities of locomotion beyond the use of the foot. The world for them was a sea of grass, and mankind was an endangered species. I watch Tim and Graham's eyes rubbering into dark recesses of the cave. Anything might emerge.

And so it did. We virtually lived a Pleistocene day, climbing through prickly euphorbias and along the onion-skin rocks until we stood on the topmost of the Moru Kopjes and could see, straight down, a pride of twelve lions otherwise hidden by the grass. Later we wondered why a cheetah fled at the sight of us, unlike all the others who had merely looked away. Only afterward did we realize this one might be protecting young concealed in the brush tangle at the foot of a kopje. Verreaux eagles allowed us to approach within a few feet. And on the return to camp, with one of the Land Cruisers boiling over, we paused at water holes and watched Kittlitz's sand plovers fly in for their once daily drink. Each of us, young and old, male and female, hoisted jugs of water out of streambeds to refill the failed radiator. By now, many of us no longer were addressing each other with civilian names. We were "Magnum," "Strobe," "Halter Ego," "Sheena," "Marfi Moto."

At dusk, we reached camp and cold beer, candelabra and liveried waiters. And for the first evening during this safari, the conversation was subdued.

31 December, the Masai Mara Game Reserve, Kenya: In four days our safari will end. I have difficulty believing we will all resume our former lives in schools, offices, studios, and vineyards as if nothing had happened. Ever since we crossed the border back into Kenya, flew southwest to this game reserve (actually the northern extension of the Serengeti Plains), we have been dodging the rains. Normally they are scheduled for November, but over the last five years they have been playing havoc with Christmas holidays in East Africa. The rain, the mud, and the constant threat of breakdowns have, over the last few days, demoralized some, but tonight I conclude that, to be complete, every safari needs an object of scorn.

This evening many complaints appear hollow. Yesterday, after all, we spent two hours with a leopard. It chose a magnificent tree to climb and then paused long enough even for the safari klutz to snap a closeup. Wendy, the poet, asked to spend a day with giraffes, and we indulged her by finding two males fighting, snapping necks against each other as if they were playing with boas. Some of us got so close to elephants that the only way we could photograph them was with wide-angle lenses. Others chose to "go walkabout" on land abutting the reserve, and felt, if only for five miles, what it is to be a Masai at one with "God's cattle."

I am going to be rewarded for all the unnecessary anguish I expended on this safari by a scheme planned for tonight: I decided a while back to scare the hell out of my family and friends, just for the joy that comes from shocking people you love.

Tonight almost everyone abides by the East African New Year dress code of black tie, *kikoy*, and long dress. Such formality in the mud next to the musky warmth of the campfire seems perfectly appropriate. No doubt we will finish the case of Moët et Chandon tonight. The four-year-old sits on her mother's lap. The only sound over the banter of preppies is the shuffling of bats beneath the stars. I give the nod.

Twenty Masai warriors, coated in animal fat, leap out of the darkness. Each has an intricately plaited hairdo; each carries a

seven-foot spear. As they advance, they leap three feet straight up, ululating, as others beat on drums. Here is the quintessential childhood nightmare.

The first ten seconds of horror on faces around the campfire are worth the safari. Everyone leaps to their feet. Some even begin edging toward the mess tent. Annabelle is too stunned to cry.

Soon there are nervous giggles, then a sense of narcosis. The safari wise-ass joins the Masai, matching them leap for leap. For nearly an hour we are suffused by the percussion, the primitive plain song, the musical psychodelia of these near naked men.

"It was the highlight of the safari," said the sixty-eight-year-old afterward, referring probably to the euphoria of brief fear rather than to the event itself. A mother and son, mostly distant from each other in the past, were arm in arm ("I never knew he was so considerate," she explained). Late in the night, long after the Masai had left, another kept shaking her head. "I just can't believe that happened," she said.

In the end, it was the ideal beginning of a new year. Most of us had learned or, at least, relearned something about ourselves. We had done what few unconnected families do anymore—we shared an adventure. No doubt, we had been hideously spoiled, but that was all right, for such indulgence freed us to enjoy the adventure beyond its domestic bothers. And, for most of us, the pleasure of having nearly thirty considerate men in attendance was a stunning revelation into the ways of others.

At midnight, as the year changed over East Africa, eight hours before the balloons rose in Times Square, I wondered what the four-and-a-half-year-old would remember in, say, ten years. I thought that if I were given a choice in this matter, I would elect for her merely to recall she had once lived on an enormous landscape where man was but a speck.

A D V I S O R Y

The Most Luxurious Way to See Africa

Recently, I put together a rather special honeymoon safari for some friends. In all, the two were under canvas for 30 days, part in Kenya, part in Tanzania, with a few days spent gorilla-trekking in Rwanda. Throughout, they were accompanied by an expatriot guide; their camps were staffed with never less than ten servants. The food was "beyond belief" and the experience "unique." Chilled champagne, smoked salmon, beef Wellington, and chocolate soufflé were staples. But the inherent uniqueness had less to do with provisions than with the luxury of being away from other travelers, for the guidance of an outfitter who knew how to avoid other tracks, for the wherewithal to lay exclusive claim on a campsite.

The cost: over $30,000—a price that increases every year.

In East Africa there are a handful of operators capable of supplying the very best:

Ker and Downey Safaris: *Box 41822, Nairobi, Kenya; tel. 254-2-556466*

Robin Hurt Safaris: *Box 24988, Nairobi, Kenya; tel. 254-2-882826, telex 25583*

Willie Roberts' Safaris: *Box 24513, Nairobi, Kenya; tel. 254-2-50613*

Bateleur Safaris: *Box 42562, Nairobi, Kenya; tel. 254-2-27048*

Abercrombie and Kent International, Inc.: *1420 Kensington Road, Oak Brook, IL 60521; tel. 312-954-2944 or 800-323-7308*

Olechugu Safaris Ltd.: *P.O. Box 295, Nanyuki, Kenya; tel. Timau 24; telex 25583; FAX 245-176-23416 (at night).*

Tor Allan Safaris Ltd.: *P.O. Box 41959, Nairobi, Kenya; tel. 254-2-891-190; Telex Compass 22963.*

Chobe River, Botswana

7

ELEPHANT VOICES

ELEPHANTS ARE BEST EXPLAINED BY stories. One story launched me on a return trip to Africa. It was told to me by witnesses at a private wildlife sanctuary adjacent to Hwange National Park in Zimbabwe:

"At first, Garth Thompson, the wildlife guide, saw only two. Plated with Hwange mud, they headed toward the water hole next to the lodge for their regular midday wetting. Thompson checked his watch: 'Spot on.' He had been watching these elephants every day for over a year and was struck by their punctual thirst. Soon, just like yesterday, other cows and a few young bulls materialized from the filigree shadows of Natal mahogany and leadwood trees. Beyond, Thompson spotted the forms of another matriarchal clan, as dependable, he thought, as Precambrian boulders. In all he counted eighty elephants. His watch now read 12:24.

"There was no prelude to the panic. At 12:25, a fly scuttled across his forehead, Cape turtledoves mournfully urged Africa to 'work harder,' shadows of clouds chased across the verandah of the lodge. Thompson heard no sound that could have alarmed the elephant, yet in a nanosecond the elephants were a beleaguered herd, screaming at the midday silence, wheeling, ionizing the breeze with their confusion. Within two minutes, all eighty elephants had vanished. The dust obscured the sun, and from far away came the sound of trees splintering as the elephants careered toward the safe shadows of the forest."

Sometime after the incident, Thompson discovered that on the day of the panic, at exactly 12:20 P.M., game rangers in the Hwange

National Park, ninety miles away, had commenced firing on another herd of elephants as part of a 4000-head culling program. Could the elephants at the water hole have heard a sound audible only to elephants—an alarm call, a cry of anguish, a death rattle? Might elephants, like whales, speak to one another over great distances —in this case, across a vast reach of Africa?

Cynthia Moss, who for seventeen years has been studying one population of 700 animals in Amboseli Park in Kenya, has discovered that they can. With the assistance of Joyce Poole and other coworkers and a sophisticated listening device that tracks infrasound, she discovered that elephant rumblings until now dismissed by human observers as acute indigestion are in fact a complex form of communication. Just as the "songs" of the humpback whale can be heard over vast stretches of the Atlantic, so, too, can these vocalizations radiate across the bushlands of Africa. We humans are rarely aware of these sounds: We can hear only their upper register, since many of their components are below the range of the human ear. Researchers speculate that there is an alarm call that is entirely below human range. In all, there are probably more than twenty-five elephant signals denoting hunger, passion, and terror. Most can be heard by other elephants for a range of two and a half miles; some are thought to travel much, much farther. No one yet knows how far.

After hearing the above tale and reading Cynthia Moss's book, *Elephant Memories*, in which she discusses not only elephant language but many hitherto unknown subtleties of elephant society (for instance, the cohesiveness of the matriarchal clan and the lifetime attachment of a mother to her daughter and of a daughter to her siblings), I decided to travel to Africa—to Kenya, Botswana, Zimbabwe—for the sole purpose of watching elephants. I wanted to find wild elephants that might let me hear their voices. I wanted to go before it was too late.

Elephant stories seem to me today like ghost stories. For in recent years, the continued existence of the elephant, and all its

wondrous behavior, has been put into doubt. When I first went to Africa there were said to be 3.5 million elephants across the continent. Today, twenty-nine years later, there are no more than 600,000 survivors. In fact, you can barely say the word "elephant" except as an adjective that qualifies "poaching." Newspapers liken the killing to a holocaust, and in recent years conservationists have concluded that no standing army, no matter how well armed, can be a match for the market economics of ivory. Japanese, Chinese, and Indians have been willing to pay as much as $125 a pound for ivory, and it has now assumed the cachet of hard currency. Extraordinary three-ton packages of awe-inspiring behavior are being laid waste for what amounts to a few teeth, sometimes no larger than a human hand.

That's the bad news. But in October 1989 the elephant's fortunes may have been reversed. In Lausanne, at a meeting convened by the Convention on International Trade in Endangered Species (CITES), the elephant graduated from "threatened" species to "endangered" species. It may not sound like much, but this bureaucratic name change may in fact save the elephant. On January 18, 1990, trade in ivory became illegal. No doubt there will always be a continuing illegal trade, but according to my colleagues at the African Wildlife Foundation, as long as the ivory ban is upheld throughout the world, such trade should not be significant. Already by November 1989 the value of ivory had plummeted by almost two-thirds over the preceding several months. One hopes it will depreciate even further, until one day ivory will no longer be worth a poacher's time and the great herds may start the long road to recovery.

I must confess that my passion for elephants dates back to the days when I, too, hunted them. Twenty years ago, elephants seemed plentiful, and my kind of hunting, short on bullets, long on walking, seemed a sure way of communing with them. "To stalk an elephant, one must think like an elephant," I used to say, and soon realized that elephant thoughts are far more sophisticated than I had suspected.

I remember one day when I was twenty-four, looking down from a perch high in a doum palm on Mbalambala Island in Kenya's Tana River and spotting the largest elephant of my life. Seeing so much ivory, I stopped breathing. Even in the half-light I guessed that each of his tusks must weigh at least 130 pounds. They were thick and straight, so long, in fact, that, mastodonlike, their tips disappeared out of sight in the long grass. Because three other bulls "guarded" him and because the light had now failed, I decided to delay the shooting until morning. I was wary: An elephant with such great tusks surely had attained old age because he was careful and wise; this one wasn't going to make a mistake. So I slept the night in the sand, my rifle coated in elephant dung. I thought myself immensely clever, especially when at midnight I awoke to hear the elephants nearby, rumbling to themselves—a reassuring sound, I thought.

In the first light of morning, I soundlessly followed the great elephant's veined tracks from where I had last seen him. For three hours I trailed him through thick bush. Soon I noted that all the one hundred other elephants that had occupied the island just the day before had followed the same course. Walking until the sun was directly overhead, I heard only the high-frequency hum of insects. I canoed to the mainland; there the spoor told us that our great elephant had left the island with the herd in the middle of the night, forded the river downstream, and had then set forth, not over the sand, where the going would have been easy, but across the Northern Frontier's flinty rock, where he would leave no trace of his passage.

Even more impressive was the elephants' unified strategy. All one hundred animals on the island had vanished. The survival of the big bull, the one most sought after by hunters, had been effected through total cooperation of the other, less desirable elephants— an escape made good, I now realize, through communication. At the time, hearing the midnight rumblings and assuming only indigestion, I had misunderstood.

Kenya's Amboseli is probably the tamest place, short of a zoo, to observe elephants. Mostly dusty semidesert, it is centered around two spring-fed swamps where elephants spend part of their day. Tourists are quite ecstatic here, because the game is accessible, unobscured by vegetation or terrain, and quite often gracious enough to pose in front of Kilimanjaro. I arrived just at the onset of the rains and found that I could drive within ten feet of the elephants, shut off the motor, focus my field glasses, and settle down for the day. For me, being so close to a wall of weathered epidermis was like discovering infinity. (Romain Gary wrote in *The Roots of Heaven*: "People feel so damned lonely, they need company, they need something bigger, stronger, to lean on, something that can really stand up to it all. Dogs aren't enough; what we need is elephants." Romain Gary was right.)

Watching the elephants, I was struck by how to the inexperienced eye they must seem at first preoccupied solely and mindlessly by the urgings of the present. I saw at Amboseli how they dedicate sixteen hours out of every twenty-four to the consumption of vegetable matter, mostly fiber. Hardly a day goes by without 300 pounds of grass, nuts, and leaves being turned out as cannonball-size dung (which then is spirited off by beetles, which are in turn eaten by baboons). They lay waste to trees at the nudge of a forehead—sometimes only for a minute morsel that otherwise would be beyond the seventeen-foot reach of their trunks. At midday they doze, standing motionless in shade, often four elephants to a tree, their ears fanning lazily like punkahs, their eyes glassy. But even as they slept, I caught myself training 8 × field glasses on their eyes, buried in that bedrock of skin and skull— I Ahab trying to read Leviathan's soul.

Armed with *Elephant Memories*, I now know that they love one another, particularly family members, as we humans sometimes love one another. I can see that, unlike us, they rarely fight their own species to the death. Under normal conditions they may live to about sixty, when the last of six sets of teeth have eroded from a lifetime of grinding fiber. And in the course of these long lives they move through stages of existence to which the human species claims to have monopoly—innocence, playfulness, schooling, parenthood, and wisdom. It is said that elephants are conscious of their own mortality. Friends of mine report seeing two of them carry off a wounded companion, perhaps to deprive an enemy of his ivory or—who knows—to restore him to health. Others have seen an elephant fondling the skull of a sibling, an ancestor, a friend, as if trying to make contact with a not-forgotten spirit. What's more, there are frequent reports that an elephant, when encountering the carcass of another elephant, carries off bones and ivory and covers them with leaves and sticks, as if understanding their value. Symbolism, grief, eternity—aren't these strictly human notions?

Once, many years ago, in Tsavo National Park, right next door to Amboseli, I came upon a cow elephant guarding her youngster, which was lying on the ground. When I approached within a hundred yards, she charged. This was not the usual demonstration that loosely translates into "Get lost!" This was for real: "I'll kill anything that moves."

Now, this behavior was clearly inappropriate to the occasion. Elephant mothers do not normally try to flatten a moving object a hundred yards distant. I trained my glasses on the horizontal youngster. It didn't move. I sharpened the focus on my field glasses: Its head was covered with ants. The baby was dead. In fact, it had been dead for several days. And its mother was grieving uncontrollably and irrationally. Only humans and other higher primates could understand.

In Amboseli I met Joyce Poole, Cynthia Moss's coworker, and went with her for an all-day elephant drive to learn more from her about their language. She is an American, having come to Africa as a child with her conservationist father, and has been at Amboseli for much of thirteen years as a researcher. Dark-haired and sultry-eyed, she seemed too beautiful, too delicate, for a life of tents and winches and punctures. But clearly she has no regrets,

for she has thrown her lot in with the elephants. I set off and soon came abreast of a small herd of cows. "That's the 'Let's go' rumble," she begins. "And then there's the post-copulatory rumble, the musth rumble, the hunting-for-lost-calf rumble, the suckling rumble, the reassurance rumble, the distress rumble, the greeting rumble, the contact-call rumble, the contact-answer rumble, the subordinate-female-approach rumble . . . the alarm rumble."

In placid Amboseli, thanks to its islandlike isolation, elephants have little occasion to use the alarm rumble. Other elephant populations, Poole confirmed, are not so lucky. Tsavo once had a population of 40,000 elephants. There now remain fewer than 6000, and that number is diminishing daily.

"Listen," Joyce said, redirecting my thoughts. "There's something more sinister about poaching than just the death of animals. You see, we've found that elephant reproduction, leadership, and common sense is *learned* behavior. The youngsters don't have it. They must acquire it just as humans acquire it, through the teachings of their elders. Language, observation, mimicry, bonding—they're all part of this process.

"Well, the elders are the ones with the ivory. Pretty soon, if the poaching continues, all that Africa will have left will be youngsters, milling about, ignorant about the niceties of raising young, stymied about where to go in times of drought, unable to lead. Poaching will create a social crisis among the tuskless survivors."

After Amboseli, I flew to Botswana. Here, mercifully, the elephant's failed immortality is not as apparent as it is in Kenya. Botswana's northeastern frontier is established by the Chobe River, a tributary of the Zambezi. Brown with the rains, it never seems in a particular hurry to reach its destiny with Victoria Falls. It delays by cutting back on itself or dividing into myriad arms or wandering up a cul-de-sac or stopping dead in an eddy. It is an elephant river: Here these gentle creatures can negotiate routes around steep banks and washed-out gullies. They can paint themselves with mud or immerse themselves completely in the languorous current. And should they wish to cross the river to one of the many islands, they need only use their trunks as snorkels and swim.

For a few hundred yards on either side of the Chobe, the land is flat and well shaded, green or brown depending on the season. Beyond, to the south, it devolves into quintessential Africa—trees that rarely give shade, water holes that only occasionally bear water, rivers no one can remember flowing. In the half-light of early morning or late afternoon one can see elephants here—strings of them leaving the Chobe, bound for "the great empty."

I am standing on a high bank of the Chobe River, watching twenty cows and calves water. Botswana, the size of France, has 52,000 elephants in all. Thirty-five thousand are compressed into this small riverine area demarcated by the Chobe and the Linyanti drainages. When I first traveled here as a schoolboy, there was no national park, no lodge, barely any roads. Elephants were scattered through a much larger swath of Botswana, and they outnumbered human beings throughout their range. With ivory fetching $2.40 per pound, there was more profit in importing vegetables than in mowing down pachyderms. Today in Botswana and in Zimbabwe, where poachers are shot on sight, the danger to the species is still not entirely greed for ivory. It is also land: Here, as almost everywhere in Africa, elephant range has been reduced, and now there are too many elephants in too small a habitat. Jammed into pint-size parks and reserves, the elephants destroy trees, tread on the young *Acacia albida*, consume their seeds, and supply seed-rich dung for feed, thus allowing other species to multiply. Along the Chobe, the effect is dramatic: the absence of almost all young trees, and the country rife with elephant and baboon out of balance with the ecosystem.

But for the first-time elephant watcher, the result is superb: uninterrupted game-viewing and every conceivable elephant photo opportunity. For me, nostalgic for how Africa once was and at heart a purist, the problem with watching elephants here was the

hordes of happy tourists. It was time for me to move on. I wanted to be where elephants could be elephants. I opted for Chikwenya Camp in Zimbabwe's Mana Pools National Park because of reports of two extraordinary elephant observers who act as guides there —Jeff Stuchberry and John Stevens.

Jeff Stuchberry's friends refer to him as "that grand old nut." Telling elephant stories, his voice has a way of doubling back on itself with its own reply ("Roight, roight. Bloody marvelous!"), and from time to time his feet leave the ground from excitement. But when he observes elephants, he is the cool professional. "That's Little Bull," he whispers mechanically as an elephant brushes against the side of the dining enclosure on its morning ramble past the camp kitchen. While the breakfast traffic between one area and the next comes to a halt, my fellow visitors to Chikwenya are enthralled by the huge, potentially dangerous bulk of an elephant within a few feet of their coffee and buns. "That's part of the chic of living right on a game trail," Jeff explains matter-of-factly.

Chikwenya Camp is clustered on a lonely headland of the Zambezi River, where the only signs of human life are occasional bush fires raging out of control, set far away by poachers in Zambia. After dark, an armed guard must escort visitors from their cabins to the bar, to prevent their stumbling into the bushbuck, lion, elephant, rhino, and leopard. For Jeff, there is infinite pleasure in knowing that he is living in country where his species is a minority.

On our first walk we sight elephants—a small group by a water hole. They have come here for their evening drink, and as they advance, the smell and anticipation of stagnant water accelerates them. Jeff drops his rifle against a tree stump and, taking position behind a bush, begins to glass the herd. A calf would like to bolt to the water, but she looks behind and deliberates. "Damn. They've caught our scent," Jeff says.

There are fourteen elephants in all. The matriarch's trunk gropes high in the air for more evidence of us. Satisfied, she moves ahead. I did not hear her make a sound, but I saw that four elephants who were not looking at her advanced as if on cue. When they all had watered, another cow lifted her trunk. But she, unlike the first, did not like what she smelled and began to run. The others, while blind to her, clearly heard a signal—inaudible to human ears—wheeled, and ran, too. Through sound, I thought, these elephants are dancing for their lives.

"Bloody marvelous," said Jeff.

I asked John Stevens, that other regular of Chikwenya, if we might find a really great elephant, like the one I had stalked as a boy on Mbalambala Island. He made no promise. But while such elephants have been shot out of other parts of Africa, a few still survive here in the Zambezi Valley. We would see.

John prefers walking to any other form of transport, and he was delighted that I shared his enthusiasm for a little exertion. Towheaded and handsome, built like an Olympic flyweight, John is religious in his reverence for the bush. When he walks he leads the way, carrying his Rigby .375 by the barrels. For almost ten miles the wind was in our faces, and invariably we saw elephants before they saw us. Most seemed to have either small tusks or no tusks at all, and I began to wonder whether elephant evolution, in response to the poaching and the culling, was now selecting for tuskless individuals.

Everywhere we went there was a carpet of elephant dung. Occasionally John stopped to point out a rhino midden or a croton tree or to explain why the long-tailed glossy starlings were massing in such numbers. But most of the time we maintained our steady tramp in silence, skirting small herds of elephant, checking the wind with a handful of dirt, glassing the perfumed shadows formed by combretum vines draped through the Natal mahogany. The elephants were probably blind to us, but when they did inhale our scent, they seemed to know we were harmless. Somehow they communicated their indifference throughout the entire riverine forest.

The next day we continued the search in canoes, floating along the Zambezi. We saw even more elephants than the day before. Some stood above us, on the banks, and allowed us to float beneath

their trunks. Others preceded us in the river, swimming from one side to another, their backs black and gleaming, the trunks rubbering through the still air for new smells.

At midday we spotted vultures, and hopeful that we might stumble onto a lion kill, we set off on foot under a perpendicular sun. The vultures, we discovered, were only drinking. Instead of retracing our footsteps, we plunged into the vetiveria grass ("I call it adrenaline grass," says John, "for it's always hiding big cats") and then skirted the edge of the mahogany forest. A quick wind rose, bringing with it the rumbling of elephants and a humus smell reminiscent of a circus.

These were bulls. One was fast asleep, his trunk draped over one tusk. Two youngsters waited for leftovers as a very tall bull ransacked the top branches of an *Acacia albida* tree. But it was the fifth elephant that caught my eye. He was not particularly large-bodied, but his tusks were immense. Deeply curved, plunging out of sight into the grass, chiseled with black, they evoked that long-ago memory of the elephant that first taught me about elephant wisdom. These were not as large—"seventy-five pounds on either side," John suggested—but they were the largest I had seen in the last ten years of elephant watching—worth $18,000 on the illegal market. The tusks seemed a totem to me. The elephant's age gave him his tusks and his tusks represented wisdom. Soon they would be the cause of his death.

One of the younger elephants was disturbed, perhaps by our voices. He came closer, searching for a clue on the wind. Finding nothing, he stepped even nearer. Now only a fallen branch separated us from him.

"Let him be," said John, turning to lead the way back to the canoes. He walked in silence. Just before we reached the shore, he spoke up. "I've been thinking about that big elephant. The Zambian poachers are going to find him sooner than later. His days are numbered.

"And when he goes, there goes Africa."

A D V I S O R Y

Where to See Elephants

Sometimes Cynthia Moss herself will give a guided tour of the **Amboseli** elephants to those who donate to the African Wildlife Foundation in Nairobi (P.O. Box 48177, Nairobi, Kenya; tel. 254-2-23235/331542). Though it doesn't take any prior knowledge or preparation to appreciate these majestic beasts, reading Moss's book *Elephant Memories* (Fawcett, 1989) will definitely heighten the experience.

My opinion on elephant-watching is not everyone's. I like being with elephants that aren't pets. The only reason for me to go to Amboseli (Kenya) is for Cynthia Moss's and Joyce Poole's research. Otherwise, these elephants are simply too domesticated for my taste. Within the park there are three lodges, all overcrowded, over-systematized, and dusty. But if you must stay here, my choice of the three is the Serena Lodge, mostly because I am partial to Joni Waite's magnificent murals, which enliven the architecture and take one's mind off the overeating tourists.

By far the most suitable Amboseli accommodation is Richard Bonham's Ol Donyo Wuas Lodge. It is about an hour and a half outside the park and is the sort of place where good elephant stories are told in the evening.

Meru National Park (Kenya), like Tsavo, has been heavily poached over the last decade. It is still, justifiably, one of the great remaining parks in Kenya for wild elephants. Here one learns how to place oneself vis-à-vis a herd of elephants, so that one can keep them within reach all day. Meru Mulika Lodge offers reasonable accommodations, well sited but rough-edged. I prefer the Leopard

Hill self-help camp, which can be booked through the Meru County Council.

Tarangire National Park (Tanzania) is a small riverine park whose elephant numbers have swollen from 2000 to 6000 as a result of "refugees" from the heavily poached border areas of Manyara and the Masai Steppe. While the plains game use the park seasonally, elephants can be depended on year round. The Tarangire Tented Camp is the only place to stay unless you can afford the supreme luxury of your own tented camp. For this, the best outfitters are Ker and Downey Safaris and Abercrombie and Kent.

Selous Game Reserve (Tanzania), at the southern extremity of the country, is a safari by itself. Ten years ago it contained 100,000 elephants, the largest single concentration in Africa. Today this population is estimated at 29,000. Still, in the hands of Richard Bonham, one of Peter Matthiessen's guides during the research of *Sand Rivers*, there is probably no better place for sensing the thrill of a stalk on foot after these great gray shadows.

Chobe National Park (Botswana) is overflowing with its 35,000 elephants. While other tourists are in evidence here, the crowds are in no way like those in Kenya. For great comfort in a hotel, stay at the Chobe Safari Lodge. For a slightly more personal view of elephants, I recommend Chobe Chilwero Camp.

Mana Pools National Park (Zimbabwe) is unquestionably one of the finest places in Africa to see elephants. Situated on the Zambezi, it enjoys an enlightened wildlife policy, a sense of emptiness, and great canoeing and walking safaris. Either commit yourself into the able hands of Jeff Stuchberry at Chikwenya Camp or go walkabout and canoe-about with John Stevens. In either case, these two are of the stuff that make legends in Zimbabwe.

The rangers in the **Luangwa Valley National Park** (Zambia) have been able to foil most poachers and hang onto about 20,000 elephants. The most complex aspect to the Luangwa is getting there. Possibly for this reason, it represents the old Africa, the one that existed before the advent of mass tourism. Here camps are small, foot safaris are de rigueur, and night viewing is a regular feature. I recommend Tena Tena Camp because it is small, the food excellent, and the guides, particularly Robin Pope and David Foot, first class.

SADDLEBILL STORK NEAR THE ZAMBEZI RIVER, ZIMBABWE

8

REMEMBERING BIRDS

I WOULD NEVER DARE ADMIT I AM TRAV-
eling to Africa merely to watch birds. It would seem such a waste:
all those miles to jot a few names onto a list. No doubt it's an
appropriate sport for an aging bureaucrat, somebody with an appetite for numbers, an enthusiasm for the niceties of scapulars and
pectoral tufts. Not for me. Elephants fit Africa. So too giraffe-like
okapis. The roar and rattle, thunder and tedium of great animals
executing monumental behavior excites my imagination by making
me ponder proud questions of existence. Birds are punctuation
points, fluttering apostrophes to life. Nothing more.

Yet, why is it that in all my travel notebooks invariably the first
and last entries are bird notes? More than once, I have landed in
Nairobi and, taxiing to town, commented to the driver at the
number of yellow-billed African kites riding the blustery willowaws,
looking for road kills on the Mombasa Road. And soon after signing
the Norfolk Hotel registry and guiding my cases to the room, I
amble to the aviary in the central courtyard to check the name of
the brilliant green turaco whose subspecies escapes me every time
I am absent from Africa for more than a week. It's "Ross," I
rediscover yet again.

Finally, after years of feigning indifference to birds, I am now
resigned to admit that no mammal observation is so significant
that I will not turn my attention in midstream to an intruding flyer.
Recently, for instance, while watching elephants at a water hole
in Zimbabwe—important behavior, I mused—I happened to glance
overhead and spotted a knot of African sand martins dodging and

darting for insects. So much for elephants as I added "sand martin" to my list.

Is this increased interest in birds a factor of age—the older you get, the smaller your field of vision? I think not. Recently, I leafed through some African notebooks of long ago; there I see that, at age twenty-four, I was irked that of Krueger Park's 480 bird species I had counted only 41. What I find even more laughable while examining the continuum of my notebooks is that over thirty years I have not stopped checking off those everyday birds of Africa— the superb starlings and lilac-breasted rollers—as if each sighting were my first. One would think that over time I might have developed an ennui with the commonplace, that I might have evolved into a sophisticated bird watcher. On the contrary, I suffer from a form of forgetfulness specific to birds. With mammals, I can become quite insufferable, dropping names like *osbornictus* (a very rare crab-eating feline found near Lake Edward). But ask me to distinguish between a pale chanting goshawk and an African hobby and my voice becomes tremulous.

Perhaps, it is because of the complexity of East African avifauna that I am forever driven to scribble lists and ask embarrassing questions. I have found that my Africa-watching is a life game conducted on an infinite number of levels. I peel away that first impression of the Masai some thirty years ago—their smell and eccentricity—only to discover today a range of attitudes and thought that substantively give me pause about myself. Waters also run deep in the observation of elephants, those affecting giants who seem to have achieved wisdom on a path quite distant from our own. With birds, too, there seems never to be a final conclusion. Curmudgeons may argue that since birds bear so little resemblance to ourselves they are not stimulating. On the contrary, I find their lives momentous. In migrating vast distances, sometimes from as far away as Siberia, they teach me resolution. Through their calls, particularly those at night, they show me how not just to listen but to hear. Through camouflage and mimicry, they render me speechless about the wizardry of nature. I can look at a feather

and feel my blood racing with the wonder that a creature's DNA can fashion such complex beauty.

In the end, the sight of birds fills me with unbounded enthusiasm for Africa. In the Texas-sized country of Kenya there are over 1,033 species—many of them brilliantly feathered—while in all North America there are no more than 703, which are mostly dull in comparison. Birds are, as Roger Tory Peterson says, the "litmus paper" to the ecological health of a land and, while larger African creatures, like elephants and rhino, dwindle, birds seem, over all, to be doing just fine, which is cause for celebration on a continent not known for good news. Even a humdrum sighting fills me with enthusiasm. In a Kenya notebook I spotted: "The view from the top of El Mau is stupendous. The hot breath of wind dries the sweat on my face. The small thorn scratches of blood on my legs are drying, too. . . . Being at the top of a solitary volcanic nodule on this flat savannah is like riding the crest of a Pacific curler about to break on a barren beach. Far below, brown ringworm on the ground denotes a cluster of huts, last year's Masai *manyatta*. Great loving lonely heart-pumping view of the world. . . . When I reach the base of the hill I spot a little bee-eater—blue-green, carved from verdite. It steadies the rush of oxygen inspired by a hundred-mile view." Great and small, expansive, diminutive—in Africa you regularly change your glasses.

That night after my host had retired to bed, I lay in my tent unable to sleep because I was puzzled by a "chwee-chwee" whistle outside my tent. I flicked on my torch, jotted down the sound, and then slept restlessly until morning, when I was able to confirm that I had heard a spotted dikkop, a plover-like bird with eyes far too large for its head. Even though I had not made an actual sighting of the bird, I cheated and added the bird to my running list at the time, bringing it past the eighty mark.

Lists. Nothing is so resented by those who do not "bird." These are the embodiment of the latent aggression they, no doubt, ascribe to all birders. Frankly, I like checklists both because of my appalling memory for birds and because I enjoy collecting anything a lodge willingly gives away for free. Often these checklists are handsome stiff-paged folders, some with winsome pictures of birds or Masai warriors or trees. The most elegant in my collection is from a lodge in the Okavango Delta in Botswana. It is a bound book listing the species name, its type, whether or not it has been known to nest in this region, and a reference to the page where it can be seen in *Roberts' Birds of Southern Africa*. On the list, I have checked off twenty-seven species and, with elegant penmanship, have added five of my own, including the bleating bush warbler and the copper-tailed coucal. Clearly, I was showing off.

But farther into the list, I see I was becoming confused. My bird sightings had coincided with a series of decisions in the ornithological community to change names that had been essential props in my birding repertoire. Nothing can be more tiresome for someone of my limited bird memory to be told, after years of practice, that the white crowned plover is now to be described as the black-shouldered wattled plover. To aggravate my dilemma, there is, in fact, another plover known as the wattled plover (or by true show-offs, as the Senegal wattled plover) whose wattles are, to my eye, invisible. My litany of complaints continues: Why must that lovely wader everyone knows as the great white heron suffer a "species change" and now be termed the confusing "gray white egret"? Why can no one settle on a handle for the wood ibis, which went from "wood stork" to "yellow-billed stork"? Get it right from the start, I say—give it a lullaby name—the pale chanting goshawk, magnificent sunbird, or the hadada ibis—and no one will dare tamper with perfection.

I do not think one "becomes" a bird watcher. I think it creeps up on you because you must know how things work. Oxpeckers, for instance, often ride on the backs of sables, those lovely antelopes with scimitar horns. Oxpeckers eat lice, ticks, and dead skin. The more oxpeckers, the worse the condition of the sable. I once saw a large male accompanied by seven oxpeckers, all working furiously along his back. The next morning the sable was dead. The oxpeckers had been prophetic.

Habitat in Africa is invariably a gauge and a reflection of resident birds. It can be said, for example, that birds have created the islands of the Okavango Delta. Imagine these great wetlands formed by a river that once sought the sea, failed, and trickled out onto nearly 7000 square miles of flat sand desert. The river's eddies and riffles created sand bars on which termites built mounds. On these exposed fingers of land a bird would alight, defecate, and thus sow the seed of a fruit tree. And when the tree grew, more sediment accumulated at its base, more termites built high rises. Before long a strip of sand had become an island filled with shade trees, high grasses, great root systems, and the pan-sized footprints of elephants—all courtesy of the intestinal tract of a bird.

Which brings me to a mystery and a little autobiography. During the spring holidays in 1957, my mother decided to indulge me, then age thirteen, with an Audubon bird-watching expedition in Florida. In those days, flying a great distance to see a bird was thought an eclectic pastime, but my beautiful mother, hell-bent on repairing the damage of a predictable but inadequate education, had determined to defy family tradition and become, first and foremost, a fine birder. We joined Alexander Sprunt, Jr., a graying avuncular presence, touring the Corkscrew Swamp and the southern perimeter of Lake Okeechobee. With his heavy field glasses, he introduced us to snowy egrets and roseate spoonbills. But, remarkably, I remember less about them than about a mysterious bird which, indeed, we never saw, much to my mother's great disappointment. Sprunt explained that this white member of the heron family, eighteen inches high with a short, yellow bill and dark green, nearly black legs, had arrived in North America within the last ten years, from Africa—flying all the way without alighting on the water. While I had never yet been to Africa, the notion of a small creature surviving such an ocean voyage, emigrating, as it were, without so much as a passport and then flourishing in the New World, impressed me mightily. Years after I had forgotten about the roseate spoonbill, I was still dreaming about this wanderer: the cattle egret.

After I began treating Africa as my second home, I grew accustomed to seeing cattle egrets on the backs and at the feet of buffalo, both of them exploiting the short grass margins of freshwater wetlands. Wherever marshes either swell or recede, there you will witness this unlikely partnership between a herbivore, seeking new shoots of grass, and a bird, goose-stepping after insects and young frogs. The cattle egret's way of life is one timed to both wet and dry seasons. So why leave Africa when this arrangement would seem so perfect?

From the start I was fascinated by the question. Roger Tory Peterson called the egret's odyssey "the greatest story of bird colonization in my lifetime." No other bird has made such a voyage. (The house sparrow and the starling cheated—they were both hand-carried across the Atlantic.) I wanted to know why this bird, of all birds, had left the bounty of Africa, how it had crossed the Atlantic, and what it had found so habit-forming in North America. My quest lasted for several months, and it taught me as much about the bird as it did about what man had done to rearrange the environment. It yielded the kind of information my mother so enjoyed.

I discovered that, in Africa, when the cattle egret's food is abundant, it will normally produce three hatchlings per breeding pair. The success rate leads to a hefty oversupply of birds, destined to fly away. Now, I do not believe we can ascribe Columbus-like prescience to a cattle egret. It does not set off across a great body of water, bound for a "new world." Instead, my informers explained, it was blown offshore by a strong easterly wind. Even today, African cattle egrets alight on Ascension Island, St. Helena, and Tristan da Cunha, 1500 miles off the coast of West Africa. If these make landfall, one can only guess at the numbers consumed by the sea.

Now, the shortest distance between the western bulge of Africa and the corresponding lump of South America is about 1800 miles. If the birds fly at 20 miles an hour with a prevailing 20-mile-an-hour tailwind, a flock might make the crossing in less than two

days. Cattle egrets were first sighted in Dutch Guiana (now Suriname) in 1877, later in British Guiana (now Guyana) in 1911, and a speciman was collected also in South America in 1937. In my research I talked to Willard E. Dilley, the man credited with the first sighting of a cattle egret in North America. The year was 1941 or 1942 (he is not sure), and the place was the southwest corner of Lake Okeechobee. He never made much of the sighting, since he was certain the birds had escaped from a zoo.

For a while this innocuous bird, its head slumped into its shoulders as if it were in a perpetual funk, caught no one's eye. Then on March 12, 1952, Richard Borden filmed what he believed were snowy egrets. Two months later, when he showed the film to Roger Tory Peterson, he discovered both his error and his achievement. After this initial landmark, the pace quickened. On April 23 of that same year three birders spotted a lone cattle egret at the edge of Heard Pond on Mrs. Francis Erwin's farm near Wayland, Massachusetts. In a state of considerable excitement, they retrieved a shotgun from Mrs. Erwin's house and shotbagged it, for proof. It was the first positive identification of the cattle egret in North America. (It might also have been its last.) All of a sudden, it seemed the cattle egret had proliferated everywhere. By 1954 they were nesting near Lake Okeechobee. In the same year, twenty pairs were spotted at Eagle Lake in Texas.

Today, the cattle egret has been spotted in all of North America, including Alaska and Hawaii and most of Canada's provinces. What's more, as the egrets colonized North and South America, they moved into Madagascar, India, the Moluccas, New Guinea, and Australia. Today, every continent, except Antarctica, is home to this African bird.

Professor W. Roy Siegfried of the University of Cape Town explained to me why the bird had so precipitously extended its range. He believes the bird made many failed ocean crossings prior to the one that led to its dispersion. The key to its successful flight, however, was not an appropriate landfall but the discovery of suitable habitat.

While cattle have been in the Americas since the sixteenth century, Siegfried does not believe they are fundamental to the cattle egret's needs. Nor can we characterize the American bison as the symbiotic counterpart to the African Cape buffalo. The wide-ranging cattle egret needed something else.

And only in this century could the bird find what it was seeking. River impoundments, irrigation schemes, and intensive livestock production have redesigned much of the landscape of North America. By controlling the flow of water to croplands, farmers have doubled, even trebled, crop production. In doing so, they have inadvertently designed a breeding environment for insects. Serendipitously, flood irrigation in North America has come to mimic the wet and dry seasons of Central Africa, proof of which has been volunteered by the colonial success of the cattle egret.

While man's efforts to alter the face of East and southern Africa have not been as dramatic, many African birds are in the habit of relocating simply for personal reasons. Ten years ago there were, for instance, at least 100,000 carmine bee-eaters overnighting on a mangrove island near Mnarani Creek on the coast of Kenya. For three months a year it was a regular sight, and I recall even non-birders being wowed by the sight of the colony circling at sunset, turning the sky to blood. About five years ago, all those boldly colored bee-eaters vanished. Where did they go? So far, no one knows. Mystery also surrounds those shimmering green Lilian's lovebirds. Recently I saw a convocation of them in Zambia's Luangwa Valley. There were several dozen, decorating the topmost branches of rain trees. My guide shook his head and said, "In two months they'll be gone—destination unknown . . . a big gap of knowledge that keeps us all honest."

(Not to know the seasonal whereabouts of a creature is to guarantee it the independence we so often deny ourselves. One of my mother's favorite stories had to do with mountain-climbing. According to her, the night before Sir Edmund Hillary and his Sherpa guide Tensing Norgay made their final, successful assault on Everest's 29,000-foot peak, they heard geese flying overhead,

calling to each other. How could a bird survive in the minimal atmosphere at 30,000 feet, she asked? Why did the geese not bother detouring around the Himalayas to conserve energy? Why, why? My mother loved not knowing, never knowing: It assured her that wisdom was also humility, that even with her limited education, she was as educated as the very learned—simply by saying, "I don't know.")

Birds at night are my current mystery. Recently in the Luangwa National Park, I set out in a Land Rover with a wildlife guide equipped with a high-powered light to see what was afoot. Now, while jacklighting wildlife is frowned upon in East Africa, in Zimbabwe and Zambia it seems to have been adopted without the slightest flutter of conscience, even though everyone knows a bright light can temporarily blind a bird and thus make it easy pickings for a wandering predator. Never mind.

Here in Central Africa, wildlife guides dress in long khaki knee-socks and professionally scuffed *veldtskoons*; they carry guns and lay the windscreens of their Land Rovers flat onto the bonnets, thus endorsing the entire operation with a windblown, rakish signature. Visitors, sitting behind on a gallery of seats perched high off the wheels, must remind themselves from time to time that their lean and tanned guide, chainsmoking cheap cigarettes, is not a great white hunter and they are not here to bag big game.

Africa, I affirmed, changes clothes at night. Bush babies gag demonically in treetops. The electric tone of bees, waiting for dawn, pours from the hollow of sausage trees. The ghostly cry of a Pels fishing owl makes one wonder whether a child is being bludgeoned. Spring hares emerge from their daytime refuges to leap like crazed kangaroos. The flat plains, during the heat a place of lassitude, now flaps and writhes with an overpopulation of these humping, jumping hares.

The object of our escapade was to find a small leopard, rumored to be in the vicinity of camp. The spotlight fluttered quickly from bush to bush, canopy to canopy. Amber eyes caught the beam and returned our gaze. To my untrained eye they appeared the size of plates. Were they the leopard's? We drove closer, steadying the light to examine the rest of the creature's anatomy. No leopard at all. Not even close. The nine-inch bird lay subtly camouflaged and immobile on the bush track. All around us the night was punctuated by pairs of eyes: a white-tailed mongoose on the hunt, a couple of red-necked falcons observing us from a borassus palm, a three-banded courser, balanced on fine yellow legs, feigning indifference by looking the other way. Dart the light across the horizon and the trees were aglow with amber bulbs, each set an enigma until we drove closer.

Of course, when we finally spotted the leopard, coursers and nightjars became incidental. Leopards are wondrous creatures, little seen and much discussed, and one likes Africa all the more just to know these lustrous cats can keep their confidence even in open bushland. But our leopard sighting was brief, and when we returned to camp breathless with its details, we turned to other matters. In fact, the very last note in my notebook for that day was of my bird triumph around the bar.

Somebody had begun one of those ridiculous "have you seen" discussions. The conversation darted from fork-tailed drongos to pied wagtails and, in a moment of weakness (because of the second beer), I admitted my terrible problem with bird names. A steppe eagle and a tawny eagle were more or less the same to me. If I was able to come up with "superb starling," I was very relieved, even if the bird was a "Hildebrandt's starling." And so on.

The assembled group studied me as if I had just confused the moon with the sun. After a British pause, they decided to save me any further embarrassment by turning the conversation to epic bird sightings. Soon the chatter was off and away, and clearly no one expected to hear another word from me. Within minutes, most had agreed that the greatest Zambian rarity was the shoebill stork. For each, it was the one bird they most wanted to spot.

Ever so quietly, I remarked I knew the shoebill well. The English barrister and his priggish fiancée went quiet. The apprentice guide licked his lips clean of froth and stared at me curiously. The camp

manager shot me one of those looks that said, "Caught you at last."

For a change, I was on solid ground, since I had once supervised a film about this particular bird. I mentioned the shoebill's breeding grounds in the Bangweulu Swamps, its habit of spraying water from its bill onto its incubating eggs, the footnote that it is sometimes known as the "whaleheaded stork." By now, I was even amazing myself. The camp manager began to falter. The fiancée repeated, "Quite, quite . . ." Her husband-to-be retrieved his Newman's *Birds of Southern Africa*, as well as his Praed and Grant's *Birds* and his Roberts' *Birds of Southern Africa*—all to check for the bird's Latin name. I calmly adjusted my seat on the barstool. "*Balaeniceps rex*," I intoned before he had a chance to say another word.

The fiancée looked at her man for reassurance. Getting none, she asked, "How did you ever remember that, if everything else is a blur?"

"Because *Balaeniceps rex*, the shoebill stork, the whaleheaded stork, is the ugliest bird I've ever seen. No one could even bear watching the film we made about it. If you saw the bird yourself, you'd understand . . ."

Funny how memory works.

A D V I S O R Y
How to See Birds

Any place in Africa is a good place to see birds—the forests and lakes of Kenya, the Indian Ocean coast, the vast savannah, Botswana's Okavango Delta, and Zambia's Luangwa National Park, to name just a few. The key to birding is not just where you go, but how you observe. A knowledgeable guide can make all the difference. Most wildlife guides do know their birds, but it pays to ask in advance if you are especially interested in bird-watching.

A few of Africa's best birders are **Robin Pope** in Zambia, at Tena Tena Camp in the Luangwa Valley (Robin Pope Safaris, Ltd., Box 320154, Lusaka, Zambia); **John Stevens** in Zimbabwe (c/o Fothergill Island, Post Bag 2081, Kariba, Zimbabwe; telex 2253); **Mike Lawrence** in Kenya (Westminster Safaris, Box 57046, Nairobi, tel. 254-2-2542-338041, telex 22992, or book through Ross and Young, 330 "O" Street, Suite 718, Lincoln, NE 68501; tel. 402-488-4192); **Brian Finch** in Kenya or Tanzania (book through Abercrombie and Kent International, 1420 Kensington Road, Oak Brook, IL 60521; tel. 312-954-2944 or 800-323-7308).

You'll be able to gather a rich bird list by visiting several different types of terrain. In East Africa you can choose mountains, forests, deserts, rivers, savannah, lakes, or the coast. If you keep careful track of the birds you spot in the Serengeti, for example, you may come up with a list of around 80 species, while visiting other types of landscapes could easily expand your list to 200.

A bird's coloring may be quick to capture our attention, but more often traits such as its feeding habits, the way it moves, and its size and shape actually provide better clues to identifying it. In his book *Birds of the Highveld* (Longman Zimbabwe, 1987), bird watcher Peter Ginn offers some useful advice to the neophyte birder. He suggests using the following eight categories to keep systematic notes on the birds you see.

1. Habitat—Jot down the landscape's distinguishing characteristics in a few words. Is it woodland, water, grassy plain?

2. Bird's size and shape—Compare its size to a well-known species and note its shape with a simple description such as "long and thin" or "short and fat."

3. Description of its parts—Record as much detail as possible here and keep the order the same throughout your notebook—for example: beak, head, neck, body, tail, legs.

4. *Coloration*—The colors you see on the bird's head, neck, wings, and tail are the key ones to note.

5. *Attitude*—This means where and how the bird sits or stands. Is it on the ground or in a tree? Is it perched across the branch, along it, or does it hang from the tree like a woodpecker? Does it stand erect or crouch?

6. *Movement*—What does the bird's flight pattern look like? Its wing beat could be fast or slow; it could fly in a straight line from place to place or dart around. On the ground, some birds hop jerkily along, others walk with even, smooth strides.

7. *Voice*—A good birder can identify a bird by its call alone. This is a tricky aspect of identification because people tend to describe the same sound in very different ways. You can train your ear in advance by buying a recording of bird calls if one is available for the area you are visiting.

8. *Habits*—If you can tell, record what the bird is doing. You may see how it feeds, what it is eating, a courtship dance, the building of a nest. It may not be doing anything typical of its species at the particular moment you happen to observe it, but if it is, you just may catch the one behavior crucial to its identification.

When an experienced birder identifies a bird in the field for you, ask him for three reasons why he identified it the way he did. That way you'll learn what traits to look for, and bird-watching will become less of an abstract numbers game, a mere competition for the highest total. Once you're able to pick up the subtleties of avian behavior, you'll have created for yourself a new window onto nature. Big game is exciting to see, but remember birds as well; they'll add another texture to your safari.

Cʜɪᴍᴘᴀɴᴢᴇᴇ ᴀɴᴅ ʏᴏᴜɴɢ ɪɴ Gᴏᴍʙᴇ, Tᴀɴᴢᴀɴɪᴀ

9

IN THE SHADOW OF JANE

THE MOST FAMOUS CHIMPANZEES IN THE world are the ones Jane Goodall has been studying for the last thirty years. At Gombe National Park on Tanzania's Lake Tanganyika, the descendants of Flo and David Greybeard, McGregor and Passion are still engaged in tool-making, termiting, drumming, territory patrols, and even war—pursuits that once seemed to blur behavioral distinctions between ourselves and this creature sharing 99 percent of our genetic material. Here, in the longest family study ever made of one animal species, Jane's research continues to demonstrate that many aspects of humanity once thought to be exclusive to us may also define another species. If chimps, she asks seductively, can reason, solve problems; if they, too, possess a sense of humor, a sense of self; if, like us, they suffer joy, sorrow, rage, terror, and despair, what then remains for the human mind?

Unfortunately, Jane has other matters on *her* mind just now. One is the increase in poaching that threatens Africa's remaining 250,000 chimps. AIDS and other virus research, in part, has raised the ante for captive higher primates. Stateside, the market for a young chimp ranges between $15,000 and $25,000. And for every chimp that safely reaches an overseas lab, some five others are believed to perish. While Jane does not now take issue with the use of chimps for vital research, she is astounded by the carelessness of so many researchers in providing suitable environments for their study animals. "We are not dealing with machines," she challenges. In one lab outside of Washington, D.C., chimps are housed in permanent twenty-two-inch by twenty-two-inch cages resembling microwave ovens. The lab environment discourages them from interacting with other chimps or even with humans; the only people they encounter are technicians who "shoot them up" with viruses. Rocking back and forth on their haunches or looking into space despairingly, their behavior becomes psychotic. "In essence, they are emotionally abandoned," says Jane. "Chimps need stimulus just as we do. How can a scientist whose kids go to school, who watch television, who go on vacations, deny our closest relative an environment even approaching the livable?"

Changes at Gombe are in the air. With the exponential increase in the numbers of tourists visiting the Serengeti and the Ngorongoro Crater to the north of the country, Jane has seen Gombe's spartan accommodations overflowing with "overlanders." The attraction, of course, is a face-to-face encounter with the chimps whose life-and-death dramas were once on prime-time television. At present the price of such an encounter is a three-day drive along Tanzania's worst roads and then the uncertainty of an informally scheduled "water taxi"—an underpowered and overloaded ferry that hopscotches between Kigoma and fishing villages on the lake shore. Since visitors to this national park must bring their own sleeping bags and canned food, generally only the hardy risk the trip. Yet these backpackers are in great supply throughout Africa; on occasion, as many as thirty of them have arrived on the same water taxi to face the prospect of sharing the ten available beds. On other occasions, fifty members of Kigoma's Indian community have bivouacked on Gombe's steep beach for weekend picnics. In both cases, according to Jane, such ad hoc tourism puts the chimps at considerable risk.

A mere thirty square miles, Gombe is Tanzania's smallest park. When seen from a boat, this vest-pocket sanctuary rises steeply, ridges alternating with steep valleys, to grassy knolls 2500 feet above the lake. Its deeply pocked slopes are tangled in mats of large, often deciduous trees, trilling with the sound of birds and waterfalls. On the beaches, seasonal fishermen have left behind huts with gaping roofs, scraps of nets, and dried *dagaa* shimmering in the sun. For the chimp enthusiast, the dry season, between May and October, is by far the most comfortable time for a visit, with each day offering a sensual balance between exertion in the humid forest and a late afternoon idyll, swimming in the lake.

Still, visitors descend on the park throughout the year and uncontrolled tourism poses a health threat to chimpanzees strategically vulnerable to many of the parasites and viruses that afflict humans. In 1966 the chimp population was reduced by a third, following a human epidemic of polio in nearby Kigoma; recently thirteen members of Jane's study troop of fifty died from tourist-borne pneumonia. "Visitors are allowed to go everywhere," Jane notes. "And they're rarely happy until they've touched a chimp. Nothing could be riskier . . ."

And once the tourists have made contact with chimps, they all clamor to meet the elusive Jane. For four months a year, she lives alone, without frills, in a verandah-trimmed house down the beach from the guest quarters. Here she attempts to shroud her comings and goings in privacy, spending twelve hours a day observing chimp and baboon behavior. One wonders if ever she recalls those early days when her mother, the indomitable Vanne, served as her chaperone here because the remote Gombe Stream was then designated high risk for a solitary white woman. Today, with fishermen poaching the park's shores and tourists clamoring for a glimpse, solitude has become a memory. The girl who starred in National Geographic documentaries twenty years ago—a delicate, shy, and idealistic Fay Wray—now has emerged as a far more complex and personable adult.

When Jane Goodall first arrived on the shores of Lake Tanganyika, her only sure skills were those of a secretary. Since then she has obtained a doctorate, written half a dozen books, and now commands $15,000 honorariums for her public addresses. No doubt she thinks of herself as an ethologist, but her most effective skills at present are as a communicator—able to dissolve the prejudices of orthodox academics who otherwise would be quick to cry

"anthropomorphism." Her passion, the serenity pouring from her cool gray eyes, her self-control in adversity, and the seeming frailty of her figure are enough to make nearly everyone she meets an ally. Even those not obsessed by animals become enchanted when Jane talks of cannibalism and war, of mother-child bonding for life, of love and passion. The four-foot-high players in her drama (she is not shy to admit) go by the name of Beethoven, Fifi, and Getty.

On first meeting Jane at Gombe, one is immediately struck by the efficiency of her language. Clearly, words mean much to her; sentences are frugal and every question is targeted with withering precision and forethought. Jane is quite capable of discussing social issues, not just primate behavior, of deferring to others' causes but, with seeming inevitability, conversation always returns to the chimps. She is not shy about exploiting her celebrity—of using a newfound friend as a fund-raiser, courier, or intermediary—all in the cause of primates.

After an evening whiskey, her face softened by the light of the moon, a more accessible Jane Goodall emerges—puckish, whimsical, even comic. She talks of species still to be discovered, delights in shocking an assembled group of followers with a bawdy joke, recounts her dreams to strangers, and points into the sky to dramatize all that remains unknown.

From such an evening chat on the beach before her house, several landmarks of her life emerge. Her first marriage to filmmaker Baron Hugo van Lawick ended in divorce and her second husband, Director of National Parks and Battle of Britain ace Derek Bryceson, died of cancer in 1980. His death was, she claims, her greatest personal tragedy. Today she seems quite content to live a life of enforced solitude punctuated by epic doses of society whenever she makes her way along the lecture circuits of Britain and America. One suspects that since she has lived apart from others for so much of her life, she has evolved a simplified perspective on people—friend or foe, helpless or useful, misguided or clever. While she is far from jaded, she has reduced her world to causes and truth. And it is *her* cause that may well have kept her young: On her face one has to search for signs of age, and her gray hairs seem only a minor evolution of the blond.

Jane Goodall's house gives few clues to a life beyond her work. In the kitchen there is no refrigerator, and her stove is an open fire on the floor. One can conclude she has little or no interest in food. The drawing room is dominated by a photograph of a chimp whose face radiates a remarkably benign expression ("David Greybeard—the most wonderful chimp there ever was"). On the side tables lie notebooks, a video camera, a tape recorder, and a few dog-eared books, which, she says, she rarely has time to read. "I've been so lucky," she says. "As an adolescent I had only two dreams—to observe animals and to write. The chimps have allowed me both." At seven most mornings, she starts on her daily ritual of climbing into the forest to make contact with Frodo, Flossy, Fifi, Evered, and all the other chimps whose family history she knows as well as her own. "It's about time I paid them back, isn't it?"

On the way she points out the stone steps she set so Derek, suffering from a war injury, could negotiate the path to join her for visits to the chimps. She carries her notebook, tape recorder, and video camera in a plastic Marks and Spencer shopping bag. Her pace is effortless and graceful. For a visitor walking beside her, there is a sense of legend in being with this woman still possessed of an epic childhood dream, on the mountain once made famous by the death of McGregor and the loves of Flo.

Within ten minutes Jane enters a clearing. In the middle of it, the tin-roofed cottage where she, Hugo, and their son, "Grub," lived twenty years ago is now gouged with Africa's inexorable patina. The cage where she confined Grub as an infant to avoid his being eaten by the chimps is now gone.

Inside one of the huts, two of Jane's local African team are inscribing minute observations into long ledgers. She greets them warmly, removes the video camera from the plastic shopping bag, and heads toward the waterfall. As she enters the forest once again,

a chimp pant-hoots. Immediately a chorus of others respond. For the visitor, the polyphony of cries is unexpected, even threatening; until then the solemn canopy of trees had seemed dominated only by long-tailed whydahs and occasional blue and red-tailed monkeys. The hoots are answered by a cascade of grunts, barks, and shrieks. Jane's porcelain face bursts into a smile. "It's Goblin." Out of the shadows he scrambles, crabbing sideways, using his massive arms as paddles. When he reaches the center of the clearing, he leaps onto a forty-four-gallon drum and pounds it with quick staccato slaps. The whiplash sound even stills the cicadas. "That's one of the ways he got to the top, became the alpha male. He learned the effect the sound had on others, when he was protegé to Figan. Once he mastered it, he overthrew his patron. Machiavellian, isn't it?"

Soon Jane moves off the trail into the forest, following two youngsters who are leaping from sapling to sapling. Unlike the adults, young chimpanzee faces are white, punctuated by widow's peak hairlines. One is tempted to characterize their falling, tumbling, teasing with words targeted to human children at play; their antics seem, gesture for gesture, identical.

"Watch out," Jane whispers. She has seen Frodo, a belligerent teenager, making for her companions. But Frodo, it seems, only menaces females. Averting his eyes as if he were bound elsewhere, he sideslips to a point directly behind Jane. Plopping down on the ground, he sucks at her ribcage, leaving a wet outline of his lips on her bush jacket. Then he tugs at her hair. Throughout, she remains the scientist, daring not to intimidate or cajole him, waiting merely for his actions to take their course. Now one appreciates Jane's vulnerability—a wisp of a woman dominated by a creature with twice the strength of man. By Jane's own admission, these chimps are dangerous; they have been compromised by human familiarity and any error of judgment could lead to an explosion. In the 1950s a local infant was killed and partially eaten by chimps. And later, one of Jane's students, an American woman, died from wounds that either were the result of a fall off a cliff or, possibly, an encounter with a dominant male. To this day, no one wants to know. Frodo now is frustrated he cannot make Jane respond. He thumps on her back with a resounding whack and then scuttles toward the others. With the danger past, Jane rises slowly and deliberately, never looking behind, her face impassive: She will never admit she was scared.

While Jane is close to sainthood in the company of chimps, there are some who claim she falls short in her dealings with humans. In 1975 four of her students were kidnapped from Gombe by rebels from across the lake. From May through August the youngsters were held in villages while their parents and friends raised $500,000 in ransom money. Within a day of the emergency, Jane, it is said, was airlifted to the safety of Dar es Salaam, abandoning the remaining students. Though she promised assistance, some claim she barely helped the survivors and led no rescue mission. Today, while in the end no one was molested or killed during the incident, veterans of the kidnapping are still bitter.

Since then, Jane's assistants are recruited out of the local population. Now no one but Jane could be a target for kidnapping. Clearly, she has accepted her own administrative shortcomings and has thrown herself completely into the task of chimpanzee behavior.

Gorilla-watching is the only other experience in Africa comparable to a day at Gombe with the chimps. In Rwanda or Zaire with the gorillas, one is overwhelmed by the paradox of gentleness and latent strength. Here, with the chimps, observation tends more to the philosophical—What is Fifi thinking about? Why do chimps become so powerfully excited when standing next to the boom and spray of a waterfall? Is theirs a sense of awe, a primitive wonder akin to primordial achings of religion? What about their grief at the sight of a dead kinsman? Is their sadness like ours? And when Passion and her daughter, Pom, systematically butchered and ate the children of other chimps, was the event unlike anything we know from observing human society?

Jane often tells a story about captive chimps to show how the line between man and beast is blurred, even morally. "They can

solve simple problems; they have good memories; they have a sense of humor, a sense of self; they express joy, sorrow, rage, terror, and despair. So where will it end?" In Florida, she answers rhetorically, there is a sparkling example of chimpanzee altruism. There, an old, allegedly dangerous chimp was kept in a small wildlife park. When Mark, a young keeper, signed on he was told to keep his distance from the "old man," since he was dangerous. Mark did otherwise and after a year he was able to groom and tickle him. Indeed he found that, beneath the bluff, this particular chimp was affectionate. One day, while feeding three females, Mark stumbled and fell. One of the females turned on him, ferociously biting his neck while another lunged for his wrist. It was then the "old man" charged. He pulled off the three assailants and sent them flying. "In essence, the 'old man' saved Mark's life."

At Gombe, watch a chimp daydreaming and we instinctively leap to join her in thought. Do they see what we see, or might the color red, for instance, be more like blue to them? Jane has spent her career puzzling over these questions. "For thirty years," she says, "I have dreamed of being able—if only for a moment—to talk to them. If we could compare notes, we might be able to answer that one question dominating our thoughts for all these years."

But such a chat will never be possible. In the wild, chimps are known to use about thirty vocalizations, ranging from alarm calls to greetings. But these, according to Jane, do not constitute a spoken language. In laboratories chimps have been taught 500 words in American Sign Language. But, again, numbers may be deceptive: The chimps' use of sign language remains concrete and ungrammatical. It leaves little room for subtleties, emotions, opinions, and conclusions. The neurological "wiring" required for a spoken language launched humanity into a sphere of unlimited possibilities—the ionosphere that will, alas, forever be denied the chimp.

To be lucky to watch primates at Gombe in Jane Goodall's company is, above all, a visit to the outer limits of humanity. When

Frodo plucks out dead scales and mites from Evered's glossy coat, Jane declares, "It's a bit like a couple of blokes having a drink in the pub, talking about nothing in particular, just strengthening a friendship." When two youngsters roll together among the fallen leaves, playfighting, Jane notes that a three-year-old chimp and a three-year-old human are emotionally and intellectually identical. And when, at dusk, Fifi sits down two feet away and glares at me, never blinking, I fret with embarrassment and avert my eyes.

A D V I S O R Y

How to See the Chimpanzees of Gombe

There is much uninteresting country separating Gombe from most of other major Tanzania national parks. The driving time from the Serengeti, for instance, is three days. Unless one wishes to divert and go walkabout with Masai along the way, these three days might be considered a waste of valuable safari time.

One option—and a very expensive one—is to charter a twin-engine aircraft from Arusha or from Dar es Salaam. A five-seater will run around $4000, including waiting time. The nearest airport to the chimps is at Kigoma, a thriving but dilapidated town on Lake Tanganyika. Here, the Railway Hotel, with a graceful view of the lake, is shabby but acceptable for one night. The sandwiches are dry, but at least the beer in its round-the-clock rollicking bar is cold.

"Giant" is the nickname for an Indian who runs a tropical fish-collecting agency as well as the private boat service to Gombe. He will meet you at the airport in a minibus and have a wooden-hulled vessel waiting for you on the shore. Usually, in the after-noons, winds whip to near gale force over the lake and there is reasonable chance that the trip to Gombe will be wet and uncomfortable. Morning is by far the most comfortable time for travel. Prearrange with "Giant" the day of your departure. His round-trip rates are very expensive and to be paid in hard currency.

The hostel at Gombe should be prebooked through the National Parks in order to ensure a bed for the night. Bring your own tinned food. By far the most luxurious procedure would be to include your own cook in your retinue, so you can spend more time in the park, swimming in the magnificent lake while a delicious meal is being prepared for your party.

Be sure to read the cautionary notes stapled to the wall of the guest house, outlining how one should relate to the chimps and the baboons. No feeding, no touching and, in the case of baboons, avoid direct stares, which they view as threats.

Be sure to give yourself at least three full days in the park to raise the odds of seeing chimps. Also be sure to take all precautions against malaria, especially the falsiparian form of the disease prevalent on Lake Tanganyika.

I predict this "rough and tumble" look of travel to Gombe will soon change. The African Wildlife Foundation will be implementing a management plan for the park. Largely as a result, a major U.S.-based outfitter is considering whether or not to build a permanent and luxurious tented camp on the beach south of the guest house. The emphasis will be to combine chimp-viewing with baboons, bird-watching, and scuba diving.

While awaiting this change of fortune, a safari to Gombe of any dimension (and including Emmanuel, the best safari cook in Tanzania) can be booked through Abercrombie and Kent (1420 Kensington Road, Oak Brook, IL 60521; tel. 312-954-2944 or 800-323-7308). Their representative in Arusha, Sandy Evans, is a veteran of just such a trip and knows all the risks.

Few U.S. operators currently offer scheduled group trips to Gombe. Overseas Adventure Travel's (349 Broadway, Cambridge, MA 02139; tel. 617-876-0533 or 800-221-0814) "Primate and Wildlife Safari" is a notable exception. A moderately priced but a rugged 26-day trip in an open-sided Bedford truck; this journey combines game-viewing in Tanzania with both a three-day visit to the Gombe chimps and a brief encounter with mountain gorillas on the Zaire / Rwanda border. At Gombe, the group camps on the shores of Lake Tanganyika and takes four separate walks to see the chimps. There's also time for swimming in the clear lake and visits to local fishing villages that few visitors ever see.

As this book goes to press, a message arrives from the remote Mahale Mountains of Tanzania, some 120 miles south of Kigoma on the shores of Lake Tanganyika. Roland Purcell, a charming well-read Irish eccentric, has established a camp on the lake shore within reach of a troop of 100 chimpanzees habituated by Japanese researchers. The camp, company, swimming, bird and butterfly watching are said to hark back to an old, virgin Africa. The catch to all this luxury is access. Purcell can supply a vessel for the long lake voyage from Kigoma. Plans are underway for an airstrip near his camp. When it is complete, one might be able to fly commercially to Bujumbura, Burundi, then charter south to Purcell's strip. My hunch is that the long journey will be a small price to pay for a unique and lively view of Africa and its primates. (Greystoke Safaris, P.O. Box 1658, Dar es Salaam, Tanzania; Fax via Nairobi 245-2-503391).

Zebra near Mt. Kenya

10

LEGEND OF NAIROBI:

The Norfolk

THERE WILL BE THOSE FOR WHOM THE Norfolk Hotel of Nairobi is just another room and meal. Remarkable luxuries and an eccentric history will be of no consequence, and they will resume their journey through East Africa untouched.

But let them linger for lunch on the terrace, for here is a Kenyan monument even the travel-hardened will not take for granted. Abutting the Tudor facade, which better suggests Edwardian England than Africa, the verandah looks out through peaceful eyes onto a roadway that is all chaos and bustle. Even if today is the very first day of one's life on the African continent, the odds are great that one will encounter an old friend or a familiar face on this verandah. Meryl Streep sits surrounded by the crew of *Out of Africa*. She is in Kenya to play the role of Karen Blixen, the Danish countess who made this beautiful land her home some sixty years ago and who similarly dined and was entertained at the Norfolk. Streep's table is only two away from where Elspeth Huxley sat some five years previously, when she returned here to consult on the film about her youth, *The Flame Trees of Thika*. Six tables down from Robert Ruark's of thirty years ago. Only one away from Ernest Hemingway's of fifty years ago.

For it is here on this verandah that time has no value, where history blends with the future, where the old faces and the past are not closeted from the present, where Africa meets in its sometimes reckless but often friendly pursuit of new values. The Norfolk verandah is not just a meeting place. It is the heart of a city that is the pulse of a nation that is the principal sanity of a continent.

Legend of Nairobi: The Norfolk

By itself, the Norfolk beggars all attempts at publicity. It *is*, simply, the history of Nairobi. Except for a tragic hiatus of two days in 1981, it has been open for business continuously since 1904, when Nairobi claimed only three dozen settlers. Now this is a city of more than a million inhabitants, the modern business center for much of black Africa, a mirror of the wealth, the poverty, and the hope of the Third World. The fact that during the last eighty years the Norfolk has played host to most every prominent visitor to Nairobi is hardly significant. Guest lists can be misleading. More importantly, it has served as home to great enterprises. It was once colonialism's club, the place where the British Raj drank pink gins and determined how to carve and splice, divide and rule a so-called virgin land for their benefit. Today it is a meeting place for the dreams of developing nations. At one time it served as a terminal for all important hunting safaris in East Africa. Now, in a world of conservationist sensibilities, it is the staging post for photographic safaris.

And while the terrace bar appears to be everyone's office, the business conducted here seems to be lighter-headed than elsewhere. Is this giddiness due to the mile-high altitude, clean thin air, and pennywhistle energy of a city lying at the heart of black Africa? Does it derive from the thrill that one of the earth's densest populations of wild game is located just beyond the city limits? Or is it simply because the waiters here smile as if they are genuinely pleased to see you? Whichever case, business on the Norfolk terrace is characterized by unabashed bonhomie: It involves lots of hellos, devil-may-care offers of Tusker Export beer, and incipient curiosity about the occupants of other tables.

A journalist recently moaned he had occupied twenty-one different beds in the course of a thirty-five-day gallop across Africa. Of all the hotels where he had stayed, he could only describe the Norfolk with any accuracy. The reason he gave was not what it offered, but what it lacked: videos and televisions in the rooms, glitzy "Norfolk cocktails" in the bar, rooms accessible only by elevator, and a computer behind the reception desk.

The Norfolk is a hotelier's nightmare, for it occupies some four acres of land, defying the laws of progress and efficiency. Management assigns some 350 employees to care for no more than 214 guests. Only if the Norfolk were rebuilt could it ever be automated. None of the four bedroom wings are over two stories high; rooms are designed not for staff convenience, but to make the most of broad spaces and refreshing winds. Stand back and you might imagine a wondrous archaeological dig; chip and flake any of these walls and you are likely to return to the year 1904.

Then as now, the key architectural feature of the hotel's living space is the interior courtyard. Two aviaries, like inverted tea strainers, house the music of this bower: the emerald-spotted wood dove is responsible for that forlorn warning of equatorial dawn. Pin-tailed whydahs and Hartlaub's and Ross's turaco burble and coo other times, seemingly as assured as we are of their magnificence. A rickshaw, a 1912 buckboard, a Nakuru tractor, and an Eldoret ox wagon are positioned in odd corners of the courtyard, settler artifacts not as successful in evoking timelessness as the bird song, a mugumo tree, and the yellow-barked acacia. The only distraction in this African shadowbox is the reckless pace of waiters carrying room-service trays.

Those who can afford the expensive tariff for a double cottage always do, for no better reason than to breakfast in a presentation terrycloth dressing gown on their own terrace overlooking the courtyard, and to peer at the unfolding day from behind their own monistella, a bush that conceals the watcher while allowing him to scrutinize the world. Failing a cottage, regular visitors to the Norfolk ask for rooms 58 through 65, which comprise a separate wing, constructed in 1937 and recently transformed into studio suites, each with its own suitcase room and courtyard verandah. Other rooms with their own terraces are the odd numbers from 413 to 427 and 19, 20, and 21, which share an ample patio overlooking the entire spectacle.

E. R. "Tubby" Block, the Norfolk's owner, was the first to recognize that his style of hotel was not what mass tourism yearns for. "These days package tourists complain if they discover that someone else was given a room with a better view than theirs. To please everyone, I suppose all our rooms should be absolutely identical. And I suppose our hamburgers should also taste like hamburgers you can buy at the Cairo Hilton or in downtown St. Louis. Well, with the Norfolk, that simply isn't possible."

Tubby is anything but tubby. Turned out in a well-tailored pinstripe suit, he stands out from other Nairobi businessmen by his determination not to wear a bush jacket in the city. His rough-edged face is quick to explode into a smile with talk of Africa's contrariness, for it is this Third World quality that makes his business so unpredictable and, possibly, fun.

For the last half century the Block family has operated as many as ten hotels throughout Kenya. Jack, Tubby's now deceased brother, and he sold their exquisite Mawingo Hotel at a loss (the only loss he can recall) to Ray Ryan and William Holden for transformation into the sumptuous Mount Kenya Safari Club. His family also owned Treetops, that romantic game perch that became even more so on the occasion young Princess Elizabeth climbed down from it as the Queen of England.

Until recently, the Norfolk was the last wholly owned property of the Block Hotels empire that had interests in other Kenyan hotels—the Outspan, Nyali Beach Hotel, Lake Baringo Club, Samburu Game Lodge, and Keekorok Lodge.

Predictably, Tubby was once called Kenya's Conrad Hilton. The image, however, is illusory, for Tubby never considered himself a hotel tycoon: He would rather have his friends surmise that he is simply struggling to make a living, just like everyone else. Weekends are spent at a converted settler farmhouse on the shores of Lake Naivasha, where he manages his gardens, which supply the Norfolk kitchens with baby beets and onions, basil, and cardamom. At home during the week, he and his attractive Swedish wife, Aino, would rather play bridge among a small group of friends than be seen with the swells that hunker down at the Norfolk. And Aino is not about to hire a decorator for the Norfolk. Every antique and painting in the hotel cottages has been selected by her.

Nor is Tubby inclined to delegate authority. Often on his way

to and from his office in the center of Nairobi, he can be seen stopping in the Norfolk gardens to remind room stewards not to leave their laundry trollies on the pathways. "He'd be rudderless if he didn't own the Norfolk," a friend believes. "It's his life—a symbol of his Kenyan birth. To abandon the Norfolk would mean deserting the country. No, Tubby's going to hang onto the place for an awfully long time."

The Norfolk accepted its first guest on Christmas Day 1904. Major C.J.R. Ringer and Mr. R. Aylmers Winearls, its original owners, had chosen for its site the favored camp of Lord Delamere, that bold and eccentric settler who abandoned interest in his English estates to tackle the adventure of Africa. While Nairobi was not yet the government seat of the East African Protectorate, these early hoteliers were anticipating boom times with the completion of the railroad. They wisely avoided locating the Norfolk at the "city center." Nairobi then consisted merely of a cart track called Government Road, a European store, an office, and an undisciplined cluster of huts, but development was decidedly in the offing. In London posters proclaimed East Africa "the brightest gem in Britain's cluster of colonies"; and touted the East African highlands as "a winter home for aristocrats, sportsmen in search of big game, and students of natural history." Where were all these naturalists, sportsmen, and aristocrats going to find a decent whiskey and soda? Where else but the Norfolk Hotel, which in one of Major Ringer's advertisements he proclaimed to be "stone built—tiled roof: the fashionable rendezvous of the Highlands . . . hot and cold baths and Billiard Room. French chef, late of the Waldorf Astoria Hotel, New York."

By 1908, while the French chef had been fired because of incompetence, every other aspect of the Norfolk spelled luxury. In a town roofed almost exclusively by corrugated tin, the bangalore tiles on the Norfolk must have been akin to air conditioning; and after the fine red dust encountered on the train journey from Mombasa, the full-length iron baths at the Norfolk must surely have been the ultimate luxury. Aristocrats indeed arrived by the

Fortnum and Mason hamperload. Even during the 1906–07 season, Major Ringer boasted there had been altogether thirty-three titled visitors to his hotel (Nairobi wags were calling it "the House of Lords"). In the Major's ranking, his most distinguished visitor had been the Earl of Carlisle, with the Earl of Warwick a close second. Toward the end of the Major's social register can just be deciphered the names of a certain General Baden-Powell (the founder of the Boy Scouts) and Captain Grogan (the first man ever to walk from Cape Town to Cairo). Clearly undistinguished! And because hotel guests like Count Eugene Von Horthy and Count Lichtenstein did not figure in Major Ringer's concept of aristocracy, they were excluded from his list. No matter: The Norfolk was making out famously even without the continentals. One contemporary observer—clearly a friend of the Major's—noted: "It is strange but it is true that the hotel business is the most profitable business in East Africa, provided the proprietors are the right kind of people."

Major Ringer, while clearly qualifying, was also fortunate that his hotel was located in the correct place at a decisive moment in Kenya's history. Rickshaws lined the front verandah, prepared twenty-four hours a day to shag anyone anywhere. Kavirondo drivers, their heads shaved to leave a small circular nob of hair, their ankles trimmed with sonorous bells, patiently waited in the shade of two jacaranda trees. Then as now, conversation on the verandah fronting the Delamere bar was of momentous events. "Here gather men from all parts of East Africa, from Uganda, and the Jungles of the Upper Congo," wrote Stewart Edward White in *African Camp Fires*, published in 1914. "At one time or another, all the famous hunters drop into its canvas chairs—Cunninghame, Alan Black, Judd, Outram, Hoey and the others; white traders with the natives of distant lands; owners of farms experimenting bravely on a greater or lesser scale in a land whose difficulties are just beginning to be understood; great naturalists and scientists from the governments of the earth, eager to observe and collect this interesting and teeming fauna; and sportsmen just out and full of interest, or just returned and modestly important. More ab-

sorbing conversation can be overheard on this verandah than in any other place in the world. The gathering is cosmopolitan; it is representative of the most active of every social, political and racial element; it has done things; it contemplates vital problems from the vantage point of experience. The talk veers from pole to pole—and returns always to lions."

Natural history, which at the turn of the century was sometimes an excuse to shoot thirty rhino in a day to examine what they had been eating, declared the Norfolk its club. In 1909, here was where Theodore Roosevelt stayed as he assembled what was then (and probably remains) the largest of all safaris. From the verandah where pink gins are still served without ice, the ex-president watched as his 500 porters drew up. Each was clad in a regulation blue jersey. Most were barefoot, preferring to preserve the smart new boots Bwana Roosevelt had just presented by adding them to their sixty-pound loads. And loads ranged from "collapsible baths to cases of champagne."

In these early days, Kenya's pioneer spirit seemed to attract and husband zany behavior. Lord Delamere, who singlehandedly took almost all the risks in the development of sheep farming, cattle ranching, and wheat growing in Kenya Colony, was no one to be crossed. One Norfolk manager who made the mistake of whispering in the seigneur's ear that it would be best for him and his party to leave, since it was closing time, found himself, minutes later, hanging next to several sheep carcasses in the hotel's meat locker. "Tarpon Dick," who lassooed lions and rhinos with a thirty-foot lariat for a living, used to parade his caged catches in front of the hotel. Fritz Schindelar, a handsome, insanely foolhardy Austrian with a mysterious past, regularly returned from safari to the Norfolk, his clothes disheveled, hair knotted, grimy from head to toe, shoes completely tattered. By evening he was transformed into the sharpest of all blades, turned out in a dinner jacket and looking the part of the consummate lounge lizard. Often he cracked up the African waiters by assuming their job, in red fez and white sash and with outrageously unctuous manners to match. Once, when he had waited a little too well on one of Nairobi's prettiest women, he and a fellow hunter engaged in a heated discussion that ended: "One more word out of you, Fritz, and, by God, you'll be dying in my arms." Fritz survived, only to be fatally mauled a year later, in 1913, by a black-maned lion.

Just prior to World War I the Norfolk underwent two noteworthy changes: It was fitted with electric lights and then sold by Major Ringer to the East Africa and Uganda Corporation. The new manager, the unpredictable Mr. W.H.E. Edgely, was to remain in that position some ten years until he bought the hotel for himself. During the East African campaign, staged between Kilimanjaro on the north and Lake Nyasa a thousand miles to the south, the Norfolk witnessed the martialing of pivotal battalions of troops.

Many historians believe those monsoon winds of change leading to the end of colonialism were first sensed as faint breezes during World War I. Certainly the Great War suggested to black askaris (soldiers) that their bwanas were no gods. Significantly, one of the first reactions to white rule in Kenya was observed in front of the Norfolk a mere four years after the Treaty of Versailles. While hotel guests were downing their heart-starters on the verandah, 7000 blacks massed on the street next to the rickshaws to protest the incarceration of Harry Thuku, East Africa's first freedom fighter. Thuku's contention that the White Highlands should be restored to their traditional owners, the Kikuyu, would be a battle cry echoed some thirty years later by one Jomo Kenyatta during "Mau Mau," Africa's first freedom movement. But at this time, the protest was handily controlled by the local constabulary with a loss of twenty-one Africans.

The Norfolk, born of one age, one race, soon to be stepchild to others, now acquired a new and quite unlikely owner—Abraham Block. No one, including his sons, ever could be sure of Mr. Block's true age. One relative remembered that he had celebrated his bar mitzvah near his birthplace in Russia. A refugee of the pogroms, he fled first to Britain and then to South Africa at the end of the nineteenth century, just in time for the Anglo-Boer War. His son, Tubby, suspects his father fought first on the side of the Boers, later for the British,

once they began to win. And so it was: Queen Victoria awarded Abraham Block a medal for gallantry. By 1903, he was a member of a Zionist commission investigating East Africa as a site for the Jewish National Home. Predictably, the then British settlers in the colony did not look favorably on the prospect of an unskilled peasant class from Russia uprooting their hopes for a land that clearly had enough peasants of its own. One account claims that Lord Delamere, serving as head of the welcoming committee, orchestrated a war party of painted Masai spearmen to "attack" the camp, thereby interrupting the sleep of the Jewish visitors. According to this account, the delegation hurriedly departed Kenya, determined that the Jewish nation would be far safer in Palestine. Abraham Block, however, stayed behind, unmindful that by doing so, he, solo, constituted the world's smallest minority.

But not for long. Soon he sent to Russia for his mother, father, and sister. He journeyed to Palestine to marry, sight unseen, the sister of a good friend, bringing her back to Kenya the day the Great War began. From his earliest years in East Africa he speculated in land, cattle, and commodities, while owning one of Nairobi's few trading stores. Tubby can remember riding through Nairobi with his mother in a horse and buggy, delivering milk supplied by his father's dairy in Parklands. "Sometimes," Tubby recalls, "he turned things around so fast we never knew what happened. I think, for instance, he owned a hotel in Nakuru for a few days, until he swapped it for a coffee farm. But he was always careful. I remember him saying, 'Banks always take away the umbrella when it starts raining.' If he had losses, they were so short-lived that we've all forgotten."

Abraham Block knew nothing about the hotel business. Merely because he valued the Norfolk's eleven acres, he decided in 1927 to buy it. To do so, he swapped his butchery and a plot of land on what is now Kenyatta Avenue for the hotel. He had no intention of firing any employee, changing the style of management, or investing another rupee in the site.

"He was not a very sympathetic father," Tubby recalls. For five years Abraham's two sons were parked far from home in a semi-council school in Britain, with summers spent in the care of strangers on the Isle of Wight. "I was hideously lonely," Tubby recalls. When finally he returned to Kenya, he begged his father for permission to continue his education. Abraham responded by sending him down to Mombasa to help in the management of his hides and skin business. Only after the Second World War, in which Tubby was awarded an M.C., did his father agree to let him work at the Norfolk. The year was 1947, and by now the Blocks had acquired the New Stanley, the only other first-class hotel in Nairobi, this one catering to business people and located in the center of town.

Tubby's favorite moment of his career was when he was chief receptionist at the Norfolk. Meeting so many people continuously helped him, he believes, to overcome childhood shyness. On one occasion he checked in Stewart Granger, just arrived to star in *King's Solomon's Mines*. The two—matinee idol and receptionist—are friends to this day. Years later, Michael Butler, soon to be producer of *Hair*, begged him for a room. "There wasn't a bed to be had in the whole town so I gave him the key to my house. You see, the Norfolk's always been a kind of club."

In Nairobi there seems to be less restraint to friendships than in the Northern Hemisphere. The Norfolk is where local Kenya settlers stay when they have to be in Nairobi, and it is not far in distance or spirit from the Muthaiga Club, the pink edifice that was once sanctuary to those settlers, the Happy Valley set, who made a name for themselves during the Second World War by playing bridge for each other's wives. During the 1940s one could say of club and hotel alike, as the British said of Kenya, "A place in the sun for shady people." Or perhaps one might overhear someone on the Norfolk verandah inquiring, "Are you married or do you live in Kenya?"

When I first became acquainted with the Norfolk in the 1960s, I invariably stayed in the "old wing," for its rooms were so inexpensive one could afford to retain them on a permanent basis from month to month. This "old wing," now demolished and

replaced with the comfortable Delamere Wing, faced the pricey cottages out of which I often saw Tommy Shevlin emerging. As a client, Shevlin was reputed to have embarked on more hunting safaris than any man alive; he probably spent more time in Kenya than he did at home in Palm Beach. It was his boast that hunting was the only hard work he had ever set his hand to. I was an apprentice white hunter, a sort of "safari groupie," and the slightly shabby "old wing" characterized the rough-and-tumble quality of those who conducted this business. Each room let onto the court-yard, which was then a parking lot for safari vehicles. One could load and unload one's tin trunks and tents right from the Land Rover into the front door of the room. Wa-Kamba gunbearers often sat on this stoop and chattered among themselves about recent near-misses. Thin walls, French windows, and a public walk to the washrooms at the end of the wing made for instant friend-ships. Liam Lynn, the irrepressible Irish white hunter, had business cards printed announcing that "Club 27" was open whenever he was between safaris. Indeed, this room 27, next door to mine, was always filled with a chorus of women's laughs, even without Liam. He liked to number his lady friends as if they were in a holding pattern above a busy airport. And Nairobi women, far from the command center of Women's Lib, thought this cattle grading system a small price to pay to be in the company of the funniest and, some say, the handsomest white hunter. Once I heard a beauty whisper to another outside Liam's room, "What number are you?"

"Seven. And you?"

"Four," the other crowed, "and working up."

On the other side of my room was Prince Alfred von Auersperg, the first husband of Sunny von Bulow. He had come to Kenya as a client and enjoyed the life so much that he earned his license to become a professional hunter—a fine one, too. When Alfie was not on safari, he could often be seen sauntering to the washroom at about eleven in the morning, wearing a dressing gown em-broidered with his regal coat of arms. Liam, the ex–County Antrim car salesman, and Alfie, the Hapsburg scion, were fast friends.

Once they both nearly lost their lives together, not on safari, but in a taxi leaving the Norfolk for a rendezvous at a Nairobi restaurant. When they gave the driver directions they noticed his response was slightly rubbery, but thought nothing of it. After an awkward pause, the driver put the car in gear and accelerated very rapidly, heading directly for a telephone pole. A second before the taxi flattened the obstruction, the two white hunters opened both doors and leaped. "That was the first time," Liam liked to recall, "the other fellow had too much to drink."

Long before my time, there had been a suicide in the room I occupied. Under other circumstances, I might have requested a change, but in room 26 the tragedy was so quixotic, so typically Norfolk, that my accommodation became my boast. The victim had not acted out of desperation. He had draped his bed with thick wads of newspaper to protect the sheets and mattress from blood, and then, before pulling the trigger, he had dressed himself in a fresh set of pyjamas and an immaculate dressing gown.

His body was found the next morning. Lying next to it was a farewell letter, addressed to Abraham Block:

> Please pardon me for doing such a thoroughly bad turn! I should have preferred to have killed myself elsewhere, but with Mau Mau rampant, I had to consider the confounded revolver.
>
> I hope the enclosed cash will, at any rate, settle my bill! Incidentally, I am not getting out of the way because my mining venture was unsuccessful. On the contrary it augurs extremely well for the Colony. And neither am I in debt.
>
> It is just one of those old, old stories: relations-in-law.
>
> All the best to you and don't let this upset you more than you can help, old chap.
>
> Yours sincerely,

Tubby is the last remaining member of the Block Hotel clan. During his tenure, the Norfolk witnessed considerable change, and there were plans afoot to build yet another courtyard behind the one that is today considered to be the heart of the hotel.

But Tubby and all the Blocks have paid a price in lavishing such

care on their legendary hotel. At 8:45 on the night of New Year's Eve 1980, the Norfolk was bombed. The explosion killed sixteen guests and employees and injured several others. It destroyed most of the front of the hotel, the reception area, the halls where the New Year revelers had gathered, one kitchen, and the bedrooms overhead. In a country that is proud of its peaceful traditions, it was the first serious bombing ever witnessed. To this day, no one, not even Tubby, is absolutely sure of the terrorist's motive.

Richard Kimenye, the handsome Kikuyu manager of the Norfolk, injured his right knee and suffered a perforated eardrum as a result. "But mostly I lost a lot of friends from that bomb. I'm not bitter. Possibly I look twice now when an Arab checks into the hotel."

The terrorist was identified as Muradi Aksali, alias Quddura Mohammad Abd-el-Hamid, alias Muhammad Haji Quddu, alias "Vulcan." Traveling on a Maltese passport, when he arrived at the reception desk on 23 December, he asked for a quiet room. Given number 205, in the rear of the hotel, he immediately requested a change to room 7, located above the reception area, facing the National Theatre, and one of the noisiest rooms in the hotel. He offered no explanation to the puzzled receptionist and insisted on carrying his bag without assistance. A week later and six hours before the time bomb exploded, he checked out of the Norfolk, boarded a flight bound for Jeddah. To this day he is still at large.

"Listen," Tubby says, "I think this chap was one of the Arabs who a year before had threatened to blow up an El Al airplane at Entebbe Airport. He and the others were caught, handed over to the Israelis, and kept in prison until their release on 12 December 1980, a few weeks before this chap pitched up at the hotel. He must have thought that the Blocks had something to do with the Entebbe raid, that somehow we had negotiated with the Kenya government to allow the Israeli commandoes' aircraft to refuel here before flying on to Entebbe, surprising Amin. All I can say is that neither my brother nor I had anything to do with the raid. Absolutely nothing at all. Vulcan made a mistake."

"I think," adds Richard Kimenye, "that the PLO or the PLFP —or whoever they were—wanted to blow up a Kenya landmark and to destroy tourism in this country."

"It's a crazy world we live in," Tubby adds. He looks out the window of his office, reluctantly recalling the telephone call that alerted him to the disaster. He recounts the horror of the scene on his arrival, and the days afterward when he, his brother, Jack, their wives cared for the survivors in the hospital. "There was one couple on leave from West Africa who on New Year's Eve left their two children in the care of a babysitter while they went downstairs to dine. They survived; the children didn't, and the next day when the parents returned they asked us for mementoes—a toy from their pram, a piece of clothing. Jack and I broke down. It was the worst moment of my life . . ."

For Tubby, it is a matter of defiance that the Norfolk was closed for only two days, that those wings destroyed have now been completely rebuilt, that the terrorist's goal—whatever it was— has never been realized. One guest, slightly injured during the bombing, simply would not leave when the hotel closed. He kept saying, "Where else would I stay when I am in Nairobi, if not at the Norfolk Hotel?" Several weeks later another witness to the bombing, wrote, "Let me state right now that I intend, health and circumstances permitting, to spend next Christmas again at the Norfolk, if possible again in room 212 . . ."

And so it continues: the hotel that outlives its legends. The maître d'hôtel in the Ibis Grill smiles when he remembers Liam and cries publicly to learn that Prince Alfie will never again visit Nairobi. One waiter on the verandah, who served Ernest Hemingway in the chair where I sit, recommends the paillard de veau. A room steward gives a mock salute to Tubby as he walks past on his morning inspection; the two colleagues nod, veterans of an inexplicable battle. And all the while, a hoopoe whistles from the aviary, a reminder that here about us is one splendid African legend that can never die.

A D V I S O R Y

Where to Dine and Stay in Nairobi

More than a million people throng Kenya's lively capital. Disparate cultures and architecture characterize this modern metropolis, but the emphasis here is clearly on commerce rather than culture. The city's reputation for petty crime has caused cynics to dub it "Nairobbery," but visitors who use street smarts during the day and reputable taxis (such as Kenatco and Archer's cabs) at night can safely enjoy this vibrant and fascinating hub.

N A I R O B I R E S T A U R A N T S ·

Cost of a meal for one, excluding drinks; in U.S. dollars:

> Expensive. . . . . above $15
> Moderate . . . . $7–$15
> Inexpensive . . . . under $7

Kenya's cuisine is an interesting and tasty blend of African, Indian, and Arab cooking, but in cosmopolitan Nairobi you can find almost any kind of food. With the help of Kathy Eldon, I've compiled a list of the best—and most colorful—dining establishments, with approximate price categories. Prices at Nairobi eateries tend to be quite reasonable, even at those restaurants classified as expensive.

> • DON'T GO TO SLIGHTLY RUN-DOWN **THORN TREE CAFE** AT THE NEW STANLEY HOTEL FOR THE FOOD, BUT DO STOP IN TO SIP A WHITE CAP OR TUSKER (THE LOCAL BEERS) AND TAKE IN THE BUSTLING SOCIAL SCENE OF DOWNTOWN NAIROBI. CHECK OUT THE MESSAGES POSTED

ON THE RENOWNED BULLETIN BOARD THAT WRAPS AROUND THE LARGE THORN TREE IN THE CENTER OF THE INFORMAL SIDEWALK CAFE. (INEXPENSIVE, TEL. 254-2-333233)

- FOR AFRICAN AND ETHIOPIAN FOOD, TOURISTS FLOCK TO THE **AFRICAN HERITAGE CAFE** TO EAT THE TASTELESS FARE THAT'S BEEN SITTING IN A STEAM TABLE ALL DAY. THE CHOICES FROM THE MENU TEND TO BE BETTER, AND THE LIVE AFRICAN MUSIC MAY MAKE IT WORTH A STOP. (MODERATE TO INEXPENSIVE, TEL. 254-2-22010)

- THE ADVENTUROUS EATER, HOWEVER, MAY CHOOSE TO MINGLE WITH NAIROBIANS AND SAMPLE THE DELICIOUS *NYAMA CHOMA* (ROAST MEAT) AT THE STALLS OF THE DINGY **KARIOKOR MARKET** INSTEAD. BEFORE AND AFTER FEASTING ON BARBECUED GOAT, BEEF, OR CHICKEN SERVED WITH GREENS AND **UGALI** (AN EAST AFRICAN STAPLE THAT RESEMBLES STIFF GRITS), WASH YOUR HANDS UNDER THE COMMUNAL WATER TAP, AFRICAN STYLE. (INEXPENSIVE, NO PHONE)

- THE **TAMARIND** IS NAIROBI'S FINEST SEAFOOD RESTAURANT, SERVING FRESH PRAWNS, LOBSTER, OR FISH WITH SUBTLY SPICY SWAHILI-STYLE SAUCES. BUT HOLD OUT FOR THE BRANCH IN MOMBASA IF YOU PLAN TO VISIT THE COAST; THE FOOD THERE IS ALSO SUPERB, AND WITH ITS CANDLELIT, MOORISH-STYLE TERRACE ON THE WATER, IT IS PROBABLY KENYA'S MOST ROMANTIC RESTAURANT. THE TAMARIND IN MOMBASA OWNS A BRILLIANTLY OUTFITTED DHOW, DESIGNED FOR MOONLIGHT DINING CRUISES ALONG THE HARBOR. (EXPENSIVE, TEL. 254-2-338959 IN NAIROBI; 254-11-471747 IN MOMBASA)

- BOOK AHEAD FOR A TABLE AT THE COZY AND POPULAR **ALAN BOBBE'S BISTRO**. THE HAND-WRITTEN MENU ABOUNDS WITH THE QUIRKY HUMOR OF THE RESTAURANT'S OWNER, WHILE FRESH FLOWERS AND CLASSICAL MUSIC SET THE STAGE FOR EXCELLENT AND WELL-PRESENTED FRENCH FOOD. (EXPENSIVE, TEL. 254-2-21152 OR 26027)

- AN ELEGANT RESTAURANT OVERLOOKING THE COURT-YARD OF THE NORFOLK HOTEL, THE **IBIS GRILL** SERVES IMAGINATIVE CONTINENTAL FOOD. SIT OUT ON THE TER-RACE AND TAKE IN THE LOVELY VIEW OF THE GARDENS WHILE YOU DINE. (EXPENSIVE) THOSE WHO JUST WANT TO TAKE IN THE HISTORIC ATMOSPHERE MAY PREFER THE CLASSIC HOTEL'S **DELAMERE TERRACE**, WITH ITS LEG-ENDARY BAR AND COFFEE SHOP FARE. (INEXPENSIVE, TEL. 254-2-335422)

- INDIAN RESTAURANTS ABOUND IN NAIROBI, AND **MINAR**, SPECIALIZING IN DELICATE MUGHALAI-STYLE COOKING, IS ONE OF THE BEST. THE CURRIES AND CHICKEN KEBABS MARINATED IN YOGURT ARE ESPECIALLY GOOD. (MOD-ERATE, TEL. 254-2-29999)

- JUST OUTSIDE THE CITY OF NAIROBI, GIGANTIC CUTS OF MEAT ROAST OVER A HUGE CHARCOAL PIT AT THE OPEN-AIR **CARNIVORE**. WAITERS CARVE SLICES OF WILDE-BEEST, GIRAFFE, OR CROCODILE RIGHT ONTO YOUR PLATE FROM GIANT SKEWERS, AND THEY ALSO HAVE MORE FAM-ILAR CHOICES SUCH AS BEEF AND CHICKEN. AFTER DIN-NER, YOU CAN MINGLE WITH NAIROBI'S YUPPIES IN THE ATTACHED DISCO. (EXPENSIVE, TEL. 254-2-501775)

- WITH ITS WOOD PANELING AND FIREPLACES, THE TUDOR-STYLE **HORSEMAN** IN THE SUBURB OF KAREN REMINDS ONE OF A COUNTRY RESTAURANT IN EUROPE. OWNER/CHEF ROLF SCHMID KEEPS HIS STANDARDS HIGH, SERV-ING SOPHISTICATED BUT LIGHT CONTINENTAL FOOD WITH AN OCCASIONAL AFRICAN TOUCH. (EXPENSIVE, TEL. 254-2-882782 OR 882033)

- AT THE ELEGANT **LE CHEVALIER**, THE SISTER RESTAU-RANT TO THE HORSEMAN, CHEF SCHMID OUTDOES HIM-SELF WITH IMAGINATIVE AND ARTISTICALLY PRESENTED DISHES. (EXPENSIVE, TEL. 254-2-748269)

NAIROBI HOTELS.

Inexpensive ($) . . . . $30–$70
Moderate ($$) . . . . $70–$150
Expensive ($$$) . . . . $150–$300
Very expensive ($$$$) . . . . . $300 and up

- THE NORFOLK HAS LOTS OF CHARACTER AND A COLORFUL HISTORY. IT HAS NOW BEEN SOLD BY TUBBY BLOCK TO THE LONRHO GROUP, CONTROLLED BY "TINY" ROWLAND. $$/$$$ (BOX 40064, NAIROBI, KENYA; TEL. 254-2-335422)

- THE NAIROBI SAFARI CLUB IS NEW, SLICK, AND COMFORTABLE. THE ROOMS ARE IMMACULATE, BUT YOU COULD BE ANYWHERE. ALL SUITES. $$$ (BOX 43564, NAIROBI, KENYA; IN U.S. TEL. 800-327-0200)

- THE HILTON $$$ (BOX 30624, NAIROBI, KENYA; IN U.S. TEL. 800-445-8667), AND INTER-CONTINENTAL NAIROBI. $$$ (BOX 30353, NAIROBI, KENYA; IN U.S. TEL. 800-327-0200) ARE BOTH NONDESCRIPT CHAIN HOTELS.

- THE LOW-PRICED BOULEVARD HOTEL, JUST A SHORT WALK FROM THE NORFOLK, DOESN'T HAVE MUCH ATMOSPHERE, BUT IT'S CLEAN, COMFORTABLE, AND HAS A NICE POOL; A GOOD CHOICE FOR THOSE TRAVELING ON A TIGHT BUDGET. $ (BOX 42831, NAIROBI, KENYA; TEL. 254-2-27567/9)

FOR A LIST OF HOTELS ON THE OUTSKIRTS OF NAIROBI, ALL WITHIN 30 MINUTES OF THE CITY, SEE ADVISORY: "WHERE IN AFRICA?" (PAGE 7).

Lamu, on the East African coast

THE
SECRET
COAST

WHEN I WAS EIGHTEEN, I RETURNED HOME from a summer job in the Kimberley diamond mines via the coast of East Africa. I suppose I was even more romantic then than now: I wanted verifiable proof that Zanzibar was more than a word, that Malindi's beaches were really composed of talcum powder, that the ships that once brought slaves to Arabia still sailed from Indian Ocean ports on the coast of Africa. Those days, I traveled with a pet bush baby, a miniature primate with large eyes and suction cup–like fingers who slept in an airline bag during the day and rampaged through hotel rooms at night. Dressed in a white suit, I bought pearls from a smuggler in the dark lobby of my hotel. I lifted the veil from one of Zanzibar's heralded prostitutes on a beach where her grandfather had once been chained as a slave. Sipping a gin sling on the ebony-framed balcony of my room, I watched swallows course narrow streets and listened to the muezzin's call, urging the faithful to prayer.

In Malindi I hired an outrigger on the beach where Karen Blixen and her lover, Denys Finch-Hatton, had once landed a plane. From there I watched a thousand jewel fish surge and parry over the outer reef. When Tiki escaped from my thatched hut on the beach to join wild bush babies calling from the forest, I accepted his loss with a mock heroic belief that Africa had reclaimed its own. And on my last evening I walked the edge of the palms to sit alone near the dance floor at the Eden Roc Hotel, to listen to "Begin the Beguine" and to admire the most beautiful girl I had ever clapped eyes on. I was too shy to do much more than sip Tusker beer and tamp a pack of Sportsman's cigarettes, all the while pretending not to admire her amber-tanned fingers switching tresses of silky blond hair. And at midnight she and her fellow teenagers vanished. It was not until the next day, on a rattling Dakota flying to Nairobi, on my way home, that I discovered who she was: a coffee planter's daughter from "up-country." Looking out at fifty miles of mostly uninhabited beach, I mused that Africa had again reclaimed its own. And to be true to my feelings, I decided I must never return.

Well, I've been a traitor. Through all the intervening years, through independence, through invasions by German faddists, intercontinental hippies, Italian entrepreneurs, Hollywood escapists —through it all, I still find the East African coast irresistible. And each year I try to return to one of five places, most of them nestled around Lamu (Kiwaiyu Mlango Wa Chanu, Peponi, Blue Safari Club, the Tana Delta Camp, and the Indian Ocean Lodge), offering something found nowhere else.

The East African coast's invincibility is a factor of its size (there is simply more than enough of it, at present, to go around) and tourists' predictability (they only feel comfortable if there are other tourists to snub). Unlike the long-suffering Caribbean, this coast has only recently been discovered by the international leisure class. In the early colonial days, settlers were not, as a class, lured to beaches. Except for a few diehard retirees, few whites chose to build next to the Indian Ocean. Mombasa was thought to have a wicked climate, suitable only for breeding malarial mosquitoes; all visitors arriving by sea caught the earliest train up-country. The first seaside hotel, the Nyali Beach, was built shortly after World War II and did not begin to enjoy success until the 1950s. Tanzanian beaches, even more remote, are still virtually undiscovered and offer, at present, few facilities.

For an American traveler, the prospect of sitting on a beach in East Africa is generally not a high priority. Why travel all that way for something available near at hand, one may ask. One doesn't even consider East Africa a beach resort, unless one is Italian or

German. One goes for the Serengeti, the Aberdares, Meru; the coast is merely an add-on.

But what an add-on: Some beaches are deserted for fifty miles; there are a handful of hotels and camps of unparalleled comfort, cuisine and beauty, skin- and scuba-diving is world-class, deep-sea fishing beats Florida by a country mile (some, in fact, compare it to the Great Barrier Reef), and, best of all, the coast is suffused by a culture altogether unique. To see only the game of East Africa without appreciating the depth of Swahili culture, which climaxes at the coast, is akin to visiting Great Britain only for its wildfowl.

This African coast has an older recorded history than North America. Queen Hatshepsut in the Eighteenth Dynasty sent an expedition to the north of Lamu for frankincense, myrrh, and rare antelopes. I have seen, flanking her tomb near Luxor, the punky stumps of two incense trees she brought back from "the Land of Punt" some 3000 years before. After her came those legendary sailors, the Phoenicians, circumnavigating the Indian Ocean. In the *Periplus of the Erythraen Sea*, written by a Greek in the second or third century A.D., there is gentle advice on how to win the hearts of the "barbarians" living on the coast of East Africa. Already there was a coastal trade along the rim of the great basin we now know as the Indian Ocean.

Excavations near Lamu show a sophisticated life-style as early as the ninth century A.D. Pottery was imported from Persia, gold from the interior, dates from the mouth of the Euphrates. And along the coast, houses were not the stereotypical African hut of mud and wattle, but permanent affairs, made from coral, mortar, and mangrove poles. Many, in fact, were designed with indoor plumbing, and often bathrooms were equipped not just with tubs but with bidets. Some homes still visible today near Lamu even were decorated with fountains, and fish were kept in pools to help control mosquitoes, all a far cry from the crudeness of life in, let's say, Chaucer's England.

I am often struck that the level of comfort that once characterized life here has once again been matched. Marveling at ninth-century bathrooms on Manda Island (near Lamu) in the morning, one returns to a magnificent thatched hut, with adjoining bath (flush loo, hot shower, big mirror), and then retires to a magnificent al fresco dining room to sip chilled Gavi, to nibble at fusilli pasta covered in ginger crab, and to know that the ancestors of these livery-clad waiters had it almost better.

Like so many coastal people, those of East Africa were invaded from century to century with great regularity. Persia, Portugal, Turkey, Oman, and, finally, Britain all left bloody signatures on the coast. What remains today is the occasional artifact: Portuguese Fort Jesus in Mombasa, the Omani Sultan's Palace in Zanzibar, the English settler's chair from Kilwa to Lamu, the Arab sea captain's chest. The patois of the coast—Swahili—was indeed enriched by rape. Along the coast, where it is at its most sonorous and most complex, it grinds with the gravel of Arabic, steals onomatopoeia from the combustion engine, lurches with graphic English, and even blends into a stew of Zulu. It is, indeed, one of this earth's great "living" languages, requiring no Académie Française for permission to steal. To hear *nakhodas*, sea captains, telling tales on the seafront of Lamu is to understand how words—words perhaps without meaning but syllables with vibrant sounds—race the heart.

Lamu is the most remote, yet most talked about coastal destination in Kenya. I went there first in the early sixties, when there was no nearby airport, no connecting road, no electricity, no telephone, and the town was under siege by Somali bandits. Now, like then, it is a small, exclusively Muslim island community. The streets are too narrow for cars, so travel within town is by foot and access to the rest of the world by wooden boat. The warm sultriness in the air, the perfume of frangipani, the pace of donkeys carrying betel nuts—these make for the impression that you have returned to a tropical womb. I remember the evenings especially —the townspeople walking the quay along the port, the ancient lamplighter igniting gas jets next to cannons facing the sea, an

ululating ceiling of swallows obscuring the Southern Cross as children dove off piers, and the great dhows, just arrived from the Persian Gulf, rolling at anchor in the light of a pale moon.

Unfortunately, there is another, contemporary side to Lamu. It was "discovered" a few years back: Fashion magazines brought their models here for "color," *Town and Country* did a feature on the snappy Euro-trash who had restored rubble into palaces, hippies passed the weed to local youngsters, and a new set of strangers to Africa and its customs converted a stretch of coast into a topless beach. While Lamu has been deflowered many times in the past, it seems now to have reached a kind of cultural saturation point. A new generation of Muslims, rapacious and fast-talking, lie in wait to sell anything to unassuming visitors. The hurly-burly of tourism threatens to overwhelm traditions, and the "quiet pace of life" is beginning to feel like an artifice of the chamber of commerce.

Nonetheless, I still make Lamu the core of a visit to the coast of Kenya. Its museum and mosques, coastal trade, and stunning architecture here and on nearby Manda never fail to awe newcomers as well as old Africa hands. What's more, it also has one of the most charming hotels in all Kenya.

I once tried to buy a plot of land on Lamu. The property had at one time consisted of a high, central courtyard house, complete with a harem quarter and a small plantation. Time, weather, bats, and the demise of the cotton market had taken their toll so that only two walls remained of a family's grandeur. Jim Allen, then the curator of the Lamu Museum, assured me that those walls represented some of the finest plasterwork on all the island. "And anyway," he said, "you have a grove of betel nuts that will cover the bills." I paid $200 as earnest money against the $1000 property price and waited to hear news from Mr. Singh, my lawyer, who had said there would be a delay since there were twenty-six descendants, scattered from Dar es Salaam to Mombasa, to be consulted. Two years passed, Singh died and my earnest money deposit went missing.

Once again I shrugged my shoulders, saying that Africa had reclaimed its own.

A D V I S O R Y

Unusual Coastal Hideaways

In Kenya alone, I count close to one hundred different beach hotels, lodges, and ersatz clubs. Most cluster around Mombasa, to the north or south. In Malindi alone, there are over a dozen. In most cases, these hotels are casually comfortable, perhaps a bit rough around the edges, and feature small beaches and industrial strength cuisine. Nothing to sneer at, but certainly nothing worthy of a 24-hour international flight. However, in my opinion, there are some notable exceptions:

Inexpensive ($) . . . . $30–$70
Moderate ($$) . . . . $70–$150
Expensive ($$$) . . . . $150–$300
Very expensive ($$$$) . . . . . $300 and up

L A M U ·

PEPONI HOTEL—IN SHELA VILLAGE, ON THE EDGE OF AN 11-MILE STRETCH OF DESERTED BEACH, THIS DE-LIGHTFUL YET UNPRETENTIOUS HOTEL IS A SHORT DHOW RIDE OR 2-MILE WALK FROM LAMU TOWN. SUMPTUOUS FOOD IS SERVED IN THE SMALL DINING ROOM OVER-LOOKING THE SEA. THE ONLY NEGATIVE IS THE TOUTS HANGING ABOUT THE OUTSIDE BAR, OFFERING TO TAKE YOU ON TOURS OR FISHING TRIPS. BUT AFTER THE AM-

BUSH, YOU ENTER ANOTHER WORLD—OF SAND BETWEEN YOUR TOES, FRIED COCONUT TIDBITS OR SAMOSAS ON THE BAR, THE LANGUOROUS KASKAZI MONSOON BLOWING THROUGH THE OPEN WINDOWS. PEPONI IS A MUST IF YOU WISH TO ENJOY THE SEA—WINDSURFING, FISHING, BEACHCOMBING—AND SEE LAMU WITHOUT BEING OVER-WHELMED BY ITS SOMETIMES PECULIAR SMELLS AND SUFFOCATING CHARM. $$$, INCLUDING THREE SUMP-TUOUS MEALS. SEE "IF YOU WANT ROMANCE," PAGE 113, FOR MORE INFORMATION. (BOX 24, LAMU; TEL. 254-121-3029). OPEN JULY—APRIL.

MANDA ISLAND ·

BLUE SAFARI CLUB—THE PRICIEST HOTEL IN AF-RICA, IN A BEAUTIFUL BEACHFRONT SETTING WITH SLIGHTLY MEDITERRANEAN DECOR, 3-STAR ITALIAN SEA-FOOD COOKING, AND IMPECCABLE SERVICE. MAXIMUM OF 30 GUESTS. THE WELL OVER $500 A DAY PER PERSON PRICE INCLUDES ABSOLUTELY EVERYTHING, EXCEPT CHAMPAGNE. $$$$ (BOX 41759, NAIROBI, KENYA; TEL. 254-2-338838). OPEN OCTOBER—APRIL.

KIWAYU BAY ·

KIWAYU MLANGO WA CHANU—TRANSLATED AS "KIWAYU, AT THE ENTRANCE TO THE CHANNEL," THIS IS ANOTHER REMOTE PARADISE OF BEACH AND BIG NIGHT SKIES AND NO TELEPHONES, BUT AT A MORE ACCESSIBLE PRICE. ON A HORSESHOE-SHAPED BAY NORTH OF LAMU. INDIVIDUAL COTTAGES ARE OPEN TO SEA BREEZES AND EQUIPPED WITH SHOWERS. THE UBIQUITOUS MATTING THAT ALLOWS EVERYONE TO WANDER WITHOUT SHOES CREATES AN INTIMATE EFFECT. $$$$ (BOX 48217, NAI-ROBI, KENYA; TEL. 254-2-331878). OPEN AUGUST—APRIL.

MALINDI·

INDIAN OCEAN LODGE—TINY, MOORISH-STYLE HOTEL THAT CAN TAKE ONLY 12 PEOPLE AT A TIME. ITS COTTAGES ARE DECORATED WITH SIMPLICITY AND CHARM AND THE BEACH IS COMPLETELY PRIVATE. MALINDI'S ONLY TOP-FLIGHT HOTEL. $$$ (BOX 171, MALINDI, KENYA; TEL. 254-123-20394). OPEN JULY—APRIL.

TANA DELTA CAMP—A LUXURIOUS TENTED CAMP ON THE MOST UNSPOILED, UNPEOPLED BEACH IN ALL OF KENYA. TO GET THERE, GUESTS MEET OWNERS IN MALINDI, DRIVE TWO HOURS NORTH, THEN TAKE A 27-FOOT MOTORIZED DHOW DOWN THE TANA RIVER, FEASTING ON DELICIOUS SAMOSAS, MANGOES, AND BEER, AND ARRIVING AT SUNSET. BIRD-WATCH, GAME-WATCH, OR ENJOY THE BEACH. CAMP TAKES GROUPS OF 4 TO 18, ONE PARTY AT A TIME. $$$ (BOX 24988, NAIROBI, KENYA; TEL. 254-2-882826). OPEN JULY—APRIL.

MOMBASA·

CASTLE HOTEL—A COLONIAL RELIC AND POPULAR MEETING SPOT IN BUSTLING MIDTOWN MOMBASA. BETTER TO VISIT FOR TEA ON THE TERRACE THAN TO STAY THERE. $ (BOX 84231, MOMBASA, KENYA; TEL. 254-11-23403)

NYALI BEACH HOTEL—A 200-ROOM RESORT HOTEL ON A BROAD EXPANSE OF BEACH A FEW MILES AWAY FROM CENTRAL MOMBASA. MOST ROOMS OVERLOOK THE INDIAN OCEAN. WITH ITS LARGE SWIMMING POOL AND CHOICE OF RESTAURANTS AND SHOPS, THIS HOTEL IS A BIT COMMERCIAL, BUT COMFORTABLE ENOUGH. $$/$$$ (P.O. BOX 90581, MOMBASA; TEL. 254-11-471567, TELEX 21241)

SOUTH MASAI STEPPE, TANZANIA

TRAIPSING THROUGH TIME

THE NIGHT BEFORE OUR THREE-DAY WALK
I dreamed the sky was filled with moths bound for the full moon,
the only light visible across the face of Africa. They flew to the very
edge of the atmosphere, high above this earth, and then crusaded
onward, without benefit of air, toward their destiny.

During the Stone Age days that followed that night, as we
wandered through central Tanzania with some of the world's last
hunter-gatherers, this dream became my continuum, syncopated
to the padding of sandals. I, too, was bound for somewhere as
immutable, as magnetic as a honey-colored moon on a starless
night.

I had primed myself to feel this way; timeless walks through
Africa take considerable planning and tend invariably to raise questions unconnected to simple logistics: Why would I choose to feel
uncomfortable for three days? What will contact with primary
people teach me that I hadn't already read about in the books of
Richard Leakey and Colin Turnbull? Why should I all of a sudden
focus attention on people rather than my beloved wildlife?

My walks through Africa have generally been conceived from a
surfeit of city. Mostly, they are planned to follow game trails and
elephant herds. They strain forgotten muscles, and at night they
are sometimes accompanied by the roar of lions. This one would
be different. Peter Jones, anthropologist turned safari guide, had
fired me up, a year before, with the notion of a Pleistocene
safari—a walk back in time to the watershed of civilization and
the roots of our humanity.

So here I am in the southern Masai Steppe of Tanzania: The long rains have begun; the roads we've just driven are mud wallows; insects, just pupated, add weight to the sultry air; and Peter Jones no longer seems so sure of himself. It is not that this gentle, handsome man has lost confidence in himself—far from it—but that the trip he planned may no longer seem such a good idea. For one, last week his wife, Annie, gave birth to their first child. He left her and Eric yesterday in their isolated farmhouse near Arusha, and none of the three seemed particularly pleased by forced separation. For another, he feels proprietary about these wa-Ndorobo he once studied, lived with, and grew to know as family friends. Never before has he introduced strangers to them, and while he does not doubt my good intentions, he wonders whether, by advertising the tribe, he may have issued final orders for their cultural execution.

The wa-Ndorobo are already approaching extinction, according to Peter. Because the 20,000 thought to exist in Kenya to the north and the 2000 here in Tanzania are composed mostly of old people, their numbers are dwindling through attrition. Among the Akie, the wa-Ndorobo known to Peter, the women are married off to the Masai in exchange for money or livestock. The Masai's great attraction to Dorobo women is not only their bargain bride price but that, being generally free of venereal disease, they are more fertile than their own women. And when the Dorobo marry outside the tribe, their traditions, language, and unique skills are almost always subsumed by others.

Essentially, the Dorobo are equipped to survive in a world fast becoming obsolete. By scoffing at the practice of saving money, harvesting a crop, investing in the future and building a convenient world for their children, they are rebels to modern economic theory. What is worse, they put little stock in the notion of a permanent address, preferring instead to move with the game and away from government interference. While they think of themselves as hunters, the authorities prefer to call them poachers. And a nomad without an address is a citizen who cannot be taxed—

all in all, a fugitive from nation-building and an enemy of modern Africa.

"Be quick," Peter had told me over the crackling telephone in January. "The old people are dying." But with all his worries, Peter had contrived our safari with the subtlety, surprise, and forethought of a master impresario. The drive from Arusha had launched us on the notion of time travel. Within an hour we had left behind street-wise Masai, tourist minibuses, and Italian earth-moving equipment that sculpted the "handyman special" look of this boom town. The road south had not been graded in a year, and occasionally Peter chose to drive his Land Rover cross-country rather than ford the pools of black cottony soil. And as we drove south the country flattened, old bedrock kopjes hove above the filigree horizon of acacia and erythrina trees, and the knife-edge heat and raw potato smell of old Africa burst through the vents.

"Miles and miles of bloody Africa," Pop had said to Hemingway in *The Green Hills of Africa* about just this country. Only a few miles from here he had stalked hopelessly for greater kudu. And he wrote, "A continent ages quickly once we come. The natives live in harmony with it. But the foreigner destroys, cuts down the trees, drains the water, so that the water supply is altered and in a short time the soil, once the sod is turned under, is cropped out and, next it starts to blow away as it has blown away in every old country. . . ." Two hours south of Arusha, at Naberere, a Dutch company, last year, had broken up over 10,000 acres of Hemingway's hunting country, and, this year, was planting it into seed beans. Some bank in Rotterdam would one day be richer—and Africa poorer.

Within five hours of Arusha, the Masai, trailing lump-shouldered cattle, appeared completely indifferent to the tourist revolution enriching their country to the north. At an evaporating lake called Ambosel, *morani*, warriors, examined our cameras with curiosity, posed for pictures without charge, and volunteered on an impulse to let me record the songs of their initiation. Like daring Whiffenpoofs, five harmonized, arms on each other's shoulder, stark naked under billowing cloaks, while another sang the lyrics in a falsetto voice so high it sounded like bird song. "It's their happiest time," Peter explained. "Once circumcised and initiated, they leave the cattle-tending to youngsters, the planning and worrying to elders. All they have left now, for a couple of years, is to roam the country, raise hell, and screw women."

By nightfall, 6:30 sharp in this part of Africa, we still had another hundred miles to travel before reaching the wa-Ndorobo. We camped near a monolith of basalt, lit a fire just before the evening rain, and ate *ugali*, cornmeal, mixed with onions, tomatoes, and bits of wildebeest. All of a sudden, Peter began rocking with laughter, a blond tussock of his hair whippoorwilling in the firelight. With some prodding, he admitted what was on his mind: Annie and his wedding. Seems the first time they tried to be married, they selected a spot next to a Masai *manyatta* (village) commanding a sumptuous view over the Ngorongoro Crater. But the priest never showed up, and the next day Peter had to leave for Ethiopia on a dig. When he returned a month later, after ascertaining Annie was still keen, he rescheduled the marriage at the same site. This time the priest was punctual, but when he reached that rhetorical question, "Does anyone see just cause that these two should not be joined together?" a Masai friend, assuming this to be an invitation to discussion, stood up, struck his spear into the ground, and delivered a fifteen-minute disquisition in ki-Masai on the perils of marriage. "Listen," he said, "I've been married and I want to say marriage is not easy. Do these two know what they're getting into? Do they understand the pitfalls of togetherness?"

Suddenly, listening to Peter, I heard a cough. It came from oily darkness to my right. I stared painfully at nothing: a clinking of metal and, then gradually, a shimmering view of our firelight reflected off two spears. A pair of near-naked Masai *morani* stood at the edge of the light. "*Hodi*," they intoned, asking to be welcomed.

"*Karibu*," Peter replied. "Welcome." They propped spears against a thorn bush, removed shields from their arms and collapsed next to us by the fire.

They had walked fifteen miles that afternoon, they explained, and had another ten to go. They were tired and had seen our fire. We gave them the remains of the *ugali*. I listened to the soft plainsong of their conversation and marveled at the rightness of this encounter. We all were joined together, it seemed, by the inky night and the fire. At dawn, when only embers were left, the warriors had already gone.

On the following afternoon we reach our destination, a wa-Ndorobo village, different in every way from the typical fly-blown, manure-plastered *manyatta* of the Masai. This boasts grass-walled, rectangular huts, laid out around a central common. Dogs hunker down in the shade and three old women crow with pleasure at the sight of Peter, while a fourth lies asleep under rawhide, her skin as life-weary as parchment. Most of the men are away hunting. Last week they killed an eland, but, over all, it has been a bad year. So bad, in fact, that they have been forced to plant maize. One old man, living with three cats, points at his clan's field and laughs. I can see it is an indifferent venture—part weeds, part fallow, and only questionably in cultivation. The old man laughs again: "We Akie aren't farmers. Look. Look," he says, spitting. "Next year we're moving—away from this spot, away from the road, away from the government, far into the forest where there's decent game."

While we await the return of the hunters, we set up a base camp near the village. Just before dusk, after weeding out all but essentials, I test my backpack, wincing at the prospect of carrying thirty-five pounds through rain and thorns. Peter, on the other hand, is happy to do without his air mattress, razor, and comb. There is no one worse on a walking trip than a martinet.

Actually, Peter, a safari guide and anthropologist and the only white man initiated as one of these wa-Ndorobo, has been camping much of his life; indeed, it is a family tradition. His father ran away from home in Kansas when he was twenty, traveled the world as a still photographer, met his wife, a Dane, in Timbuktu. Peter, born in Germany near the Leica plant, spent his first months in a make-shift crib in a Volkswagen bus, being driven to Afghanistan, where he was the youngest European child to set foot in the Hindu Kush. When he was twelve, he observed a demonstration of stone tool-making in Denmark and tried to do it himself. By age fourteen he was working as Professor Borde's fellow flint-knapper in the Cro-Magnon sites of France's Dordogne Valley. By age eighteen he had so impressed the anthropologist Kenneth Oakley that he was given a letter of introduction to Mary Leakey, Louis' widow and Richard's mother. This piece of paper brought him to Africa and for the next eight years he contributed to Dr. Leakey's stone tool research in the Olduvai Gorge of Tanzania. Some say Peter, at age thirty-three, is today among a handful of the world's finest stone toolmakers. "It's amazing nonetheless," he says, dismissing the praise as utter nonsense, "that I, one of the world's worst students, actually made it as far as here. I can remember dreaming in physics class about living, one day, in Africa. What's happened far exceeds my dreams."

Just before dark a dog called Lubi tells us of the hunters' return. He is lean and spotted and would have been dismissed as a mutt anywhere but here. He sniffs the Land Rover, eyes our pale skins with learned suspicion, and then trots away to tell his master. "He belongs to Kirripe," says Peter, "and he's one of the best hunters around."

The hunters and the women appear at dusk. At first part shadow, part movement, they approach us like a soft wind. I only become aware of them filling our camp the instant they clap eyes on Peter. A year has passed since they last saw him, but out here, as he later explains, long absences rarely threaten friendships. For Kirripe, the sight of Peter ("Pitah") is laughter itself. His teeth glisten in the dark and his skin seems more blue than black. In these shadows, Kirripe's face becomes a roadmap to the moment, with the fine skin drawn and every artery visible and the blood pumping

fast with pleasure. Not just teeth and eyes are transformed, but the entire face becomes a jigsaw of lost control. And when he hears of "Pitah's" newborn—best of all, a male—the joy becomes a personal compliment. "*Asante. Asante*," he says. "Thank you. Thank you."

Kelta is another matter altogether. Tall and bent, he seems to have been born old. His earlobes are pierced, and the resulting loops are like sun-softened licorice. Each of his eyebrows has been rearranged by machete fights, and his nose seems only half there. ("His brother once tried to bite it off," Peter explained.) Kelta arrives at our clearing walking a blind man on a stick, one the dog and the other its master. Even with the stick, the blind man falls into bushes, hits trees, and trips in holes, for Kelta seems more engaged in sizing us up than in helping his friend. "He's blind," Kelta whispers theatrically. He puts his finger to his lips to remind me of my manners.

"Careful," mutters Peter. "That's 'Old Shitface'—Annie's term—and he's trouble. He'll always want something from you, and he's never satisfied." In one way, it is from Kelta I learn the most.

The others leap at the mention of a safari. Joji, dour but agreeable, falls in with the general consensus. It is agreed: A giraffe has been killed by another clan about twelve miles away, and there must be plenty of meat left over for this village. We shall walk there and see what turns up.

At dawn the next morning an old woman, her face yellowed and creased like a Bushman's, squats beside our fire, drinking tea, observing our departure bemusedly. I make my first step. A thirty-five-pound pack! As I follow the others, I play with it, jacking it up from the bottom one minute, tucking my thumbs under the harness another, wondering all the while how the professionals do it. Flies circle us and a dove plinks metallically. Soon my shirt is drenched from perspiration, and the distance between the last in line and myself widens.

The wa-Ndorobo barely carry anything. Their portable belongings amount to a bow, a quiver filled with poisoned arrows, a hatchet, and a rawhide honey container resembling a small golfbag. I doubt whether their load weighs more than five pounds. But even unencumbered, I am struck by how they maintain such a steady pace, dodging thorns with educated eyes, while I flounder from one bush to the next, ripping my shirt and flailing my bare legs until they are ribboned with blood. Their skin, seemingly so delicate, appears immune to thorns. Even more impressive: their calves, knotted with arteries and almost completely innocent of muscles. Seen from the waist up, these wa-Ndorobo move as if on wheels.

In this country, the most direct route between two points is not in a straight line but from water to water. The country is flat, dominated by only occasional hills, and the best landmarks are invariably the tortured baobab trees and the water holes—each one of meaning to the wa-Ndorobo. After two hours, when I begin wondering how to steel myself to ask one of the hunters to help with my load, we come to a water hole the size of a small lake. Lubi makes straight for it without any preliminaries. Kelta draws a thin metal tube out of his quiver; in the middle of the lake he plunges it to the bottom and sucks out the cool water. The spareness of their needs, matched by simple belongings, have created a life of supreme natural elegance.

In addition to arrows and water tubes, each of our companions' quivers contains a "magic stick"—essential baggage on any of their safaris. Throughout East Africa the wa-Ndorobo are known for their sorcery and often are solicited by other tribes for help against wild animals. Ashes from the "magic stick," burned at one end, can be scattered around a camp at night, even if it is right on a game trail. "Stay away buffalo, elephants, rhino, and lion," they will intone and, according to Peter, even the hungriest man-eater will avoid the camp. Equally, when an elephant has been killed, ashes from the "magic stick" will deter birds of prey. "Listen," says Peter, as I gulp tepid water out of my canteen, "I'd say a lot of their magic amounts only to damn good bushcraft. They're in

demand by other tribes because they know so many of the fundamentals of animal lore. Still . . ." I pass him the canteen. "Still, I've seen magic myself."

The wa-Ndorobo, Peter explains, have a reputation for disappearing. Twice, when hunting with them, Masai stalked past a hundred feet away and never saw them, even though they made no special effort to conceal themselves. When questioned about this later, the wa-Ndorobo replied, "When we don't want to be seen, we aren't."

For the wa-Ndorobo, empirical evidence is not the final authority. To them, mythology is real, anomalies to reality abound, and mysteries need never be plumbed. This water hole, for instance, looks man-made, according to Peter. Its walls have been carefully carved, and the sloping banks are ringed by earthworks. Because it is so large, one assumes its creators must have been livestock herders. "Who made this water hole?" Peter asks Kirripe.

"The wa-Reno," he replies.

"Who were they? When did they live?"

Kirripe shrugs. "Long ago. Long before even our ancestors arrived." He seems at peace with the mystery. He spits and continues walking.

11:19: "Sleeping bag ripped off my pack by these bloody thorns. Only noticed loss after a quarter of a mile, retraced steps, found it and then repacked. Have just diverted to visit an erythrina tree. Joji climbs to a central crotch where rainwater has collected. A small wooden bowl floats on the surface. He explains it is the collective property of all wa-Ndorobo, and this tree, unmarked and undistinguished, is the equivalent of a major truck stop. After all the men have drunk, Joji climbs down and offers the cup to Lubi, the dog."

12:34: "Sweat bees swarm at the edge of my eyes. They have no sting but are a nuisance since they don't respond to swats. Theirs is said to be the best honey of all."

13:01: "Blisters on both heels. When I fall down a warthog hole, Joji rushes up, saying 'sorry, sorry' as if he had been responsible for the hole. Bush is almost impenetrable. We no longer follow elephant trails but make our own. I can see for only a few feet. Defies reason how these men know where they are."

14:19: "Sweet smell of rotting meat tells me we've arrived. Behind a bush old men squat. A fire burns and the smoke trails into the overcast sky. Dozens of long meat strips hang from branches to smoke and dry. Kirripe's woman stirs a pot, her cloak lowered, exposing two flat breasts. Old men gnaw on joints. In spite of the flies, chronic even at a distance of fifty feet, and the scarab beetles, rolling dungballs, the dominant sound is the soft murmur of contentment."

I am witnessing, I think, a re-enactment of a Stone Age scene. It defies everything our society counts as sacred—legal hunting, royal game, well-preserved meat. These men, reason dictates, are risking life and independence for their way of life. Clearly, they see the issue otherwise. Hunting with bows and arrows is their definition of freedom.

In late afternoon, I join Joji, who follows a honey guide. The bird has been rasping overhead for the last hour, and now it leads us into thick bush to an erythrina tree. Joji sticks smoking leaves into a waist-high hole and, as the bees pour out, he enlarges another one farther up the tree. Eventually he is able to reach in and bring out a sticky comb of larvae. By sunset we are laden with spoils. Joji deposits a hunk of larvae on the ground as reward for the bird. "Must never leave too much," he explains. "Otherwise these birds won't help other Dorobo."

"These people are on 'the six-week survival plan,'" explains Peter that night in our camp, purposefully sited upwind from theirs. "In six weeks they're dead if they don't hunt. Sure, if they luck into a cache of honey, they'll make buckets of beer and they'll be on the piss for days, but it's meat that keeps them alive. And money—they treat that like meat, too: If you keep it too long, it'll spoil . . .

"When I first came here," Peter continues, "I thought this was the life—a little hunting here, good drink, and lounging around

with the women the rest of the time. Well, that's not the way it is. There's anxiety here, just like in the West. You can never be too relaxed if you know you've only got six weeks to live."

Two hyenas, lured by the rank smell, yip from far away, and Lubi responds with a threatening growl. With darkness the flies have vanished and the fire, snapping the dry acacia wood, sends smoke fluking through the canopy of leaves. I think to myself: I have just aided and abetted "poachers." These are the monsters I once had hoped my donations to conservation would put behind bars. Yet, are they an honest risk? One giraffe killed with a bow and arrow will now feed about sixty people for nearly two weeks and will keep these people, during that time, from the need to kill anything else. Are these master hunters the real monsters threatening wildlife? Kirripe this afternoon, while stropping a strip of giraffe hide, noticed he was keeping a brilliantly feathered hoopoe from returning to her nest. Without a word, he, the greatest "killer" of all these wa-Ndorobo, removed his strop from the tree and watched her feed her young.

In the morning our departure is slow. Lubi barked all night at the hyenas, keeping us from sleep. Now strips of game meat are bundled like asparagus, wrapped in bohenia vines, and slung on rawhide straps from the hunters' foreheads. Our progress is decidedly slower than yesterday's. To follow the hunters is to contend with the encircling flies and powerful odors—decaying meat both in and out of the intestinal tract. But to lead is perilous. I am not even sure where we are heading—a water hole lost in the collective unconscious. Our path willowaws from bush to bush.

After four hours we come upon Masai cattle. Naked boys ululate at a distance and dash to head off a stampede. A lone warrior stands waiting to greet us and invites us back to his *manyatta* to exhibit us to his wives. The wa-Ndorobo seem to be excluded from this invitation—no slight at all, since they are loathe to add Masai flies to their own. The Masai were indeed the ones who coined the wa-Ndorobos' name. In Masai, *il torobo* means poor people. Cattle—even at the price of manure and flies—is for the Masai the earth's only currency of value. Those who hunt wild animals for survival are condemned to a kind of moral insolvency.

With the *manyatta* far behind, Peter tells me that even the wa-Ndorobo sustain this legend. Kirripe once told him that his people's lot was established when God set the first Masai and the first wa-Ndorobo on the earth. Each was given a leather bag, told to go home, cut a big clearing where he was to open the bag. Out of it, each was told, would come his livelihood. The Masai trotted home, made a huge thorn fence, cleared the area in the center and opened the bag. Out leaped a herd of cattle. "Well," said Kirripe, "you know how dumb Dorobo are—this one, walking home, began to wonder what ever could be inside the bag. He didn't like the idea of chopping down all those trees, so he just stopped on the path and opened the bag. Out sprang wild animals, and he's been forced to harvest them ever since. Have you ever heard anything so stupid?"

There is little honey to be found in the baobab trees. Each time the track takes us close to one of these landmarks, we lie back on our loads while awaiting Joji's report. Invariably, he returns, his eyes solemn and unreadable. The rains, he explains, are not sufficiently advanced for the production of nectar. On the march, Kirripe prods elephant dung with his knuckles. "Yesterday, late afternoon," he mutters quietly. Giraffe, too, have bisected our path just before dawn. Hyenas have preceded us on this path by only a half hour and I can see where they have urinated against the wild hibiscus. Once, with his long elegant finger scratching the dirt, Kirripe illustrates the ephemeral difference between sable, kongoni, and wildebeest tracks. He laughs quietly, saying that even the Masai can't make the distinction. Still, he seems surprised that any white man would yearn for this knowledge. By prying, I discover each bush has a name and a function. Nothing, I learn, is for naught.

By two, when we reach the vaunted water hole, I am not nearly as tired as I was this time yesterday. Only blisters can slow me down now. Kirripe and the others repossess an abandoned Masai

manyatta, while we set our fly and groundsheet upwind, under a lone acacia. All the while I can hear Kirripe muttering to the others; he is angry, for Kelta and his woman lingered on this morning's path and now have not arrived. "Ever since he was born, Kelta's been stupid," I can hear Kirripe excoriating. "Imagine, getting lost in this country."

On the other hand, I have difficulty finding the water hole, only a quarter of a mile away. There, as night falls, Peter and I sit on a worn rock, cooling steamed feet and watching a pair of Egyptian geese strut on the far bank. Only a few minutes before, Kelta and his woman had arrived in camp. Drawn and thirsty, the old man with the licorice lobes had sat down by the fire, looking wizened. Clearly, it was unthinkable for a m-Ndorobo to lose his way in the country of his birth. But no sooner had he recovered his spirits than he began arguing with me that I would owe him lots of money for all the pictures I had taken. Kirripe listened remotely and then made a limp-handed gesture of disdain.

Now, on the edge of the pool, with swallows crisscrossing the surface after a new hatch of insects, Peter recalls a memory of Kelta: every day making a display of sharpening his arrows and setting off for the hunt, every day returning empty-handed. Once, long ago, when Peter organized an archery contest, he discovered that Kelta could not even see the target, let alone hit it.

While Kirripe is an authoritative hunter who continues learning, a decent man in any society, it is Kelta, mean-spirited and dim, inefficient and cowardly, whose life best silhouettes the precariousness of the wa-Ndorobo's existence. After only three days he has exposed every one of his failings. Anywhere else the Keltas of the world might have concealed them behind artifice. Here there is no cultural camouflage. In these green hills of Africa where a human's future is never more certain than six weeks, failures are very real and the wobbles of personality are etched deep.

The following day is our last. Five hours of walking separate us from base camp and now veldt sores, not blisters, become our primary source of discomfort. These are nothing more than thorn scratches infected by the morning dew, but since I have been wearing shorts, whole sections of my calves are beribboned by proud flesh. From time to time Kirripe stops, too, suffering from a broken strap on his sandals. And with each stop he rolls his eyes to announce he has another "punkcha"—a joke, no doubt, intended to span his world and mine.

Occasionally, on this final march, the hunters draw arrows from their quivers and, with Lubi's tail flailing the high grass, stalk from bush to bush: It is only play-acting and the game is imaginary. But in proving the strength of their bow arms, the potency of their poison, they are making, I think, a desperate point: This country is changing and today there are too many competitors for the game. Next year, over and over they intone, they will leave their village and move "far from roads, far from other people, deep into the forest."

As we approach their village, the game trail evolves into a proper track and, for the first time in three days, I can walk a straight line. We are almost home but Kirripe has not finished. Along this easy trail, he has been telling us his long-ago memories from the days he worked as a tracker for a white hunter. He looks up at the sky, building with thunderheads. "Look," he says, pointing at a dot, dodging through gaps in the clouds. "Once, then, I traveled in an airplane just like that." We can see Kirripe is proud of this story; already I have begun to smile. "And you know, we even flew *above* the clouds." Now he is ecstatic, his teeth radiantly white and the blood visibly pulsing through an artery on his neck. "And do you know what we found *above* the clouds?" Peter and I both shake our heads. ". . . More clouds . . ."

So too with me, wandering with wa-Ndorobo.

OKAVANGO DELTA, BOTSWANA

A D V I S O R Y

How to Walk into the Stone Age

- BY FAR THE MOST KNOWLEDGEABLE AND COMPANION-
ABLE OF ALL GUIDES IN THE SPHERE OF ANTHROPOLOGY
IS **PETER JONES**. HE CAN TAKE YOU TO VISIT VARIOUS
HUNTER-GATHERS AND THE MASAI TRIBESMEN. THE COST
CAN VARY, BUT STARTS $240 PER DAY PER PERSON. (P.O.
BOX 49, ARUSHA, TANZANIA; IN THE U.S., YOU CAN BOOK
SOME OF HIS TRIPS THROUGH ABERCROMBIE AND KENT
INTERNATIONAL, 1420 KENSINGTON ROAD, OAK BROOK,
IL 60521; TEL. 312-954-2944 OR 800-323-7308. OTH-
ERS CAN BE ARRANGED THROUGH ANNE KENT TAYLOR
OF A.K. TAYLOR INTERNATIONAL, 2724 ARVIN ROAD,
BILLINGS, MT 59102; TEL. 406-656-0706.)

- **DAVE PETERSON**, OF DOROBO TOURS AND SAFARIS, ALSO
LEADS WALKING SAFARIS. THESE FOCUS ON THE MASAI.
(BOX 2534, ARUSHA, TANZANIA; TELEX 42018)

- TO MEET SOME OF NORTHERN KENYA'S MOST INTEREST-
ING TRIBES, CONTACT **CHRISSIE ALDRICH** OF FLAME TREE
SAFARIS. FROM HER SUMPTUOUS CAMP IN THE MATHEWS
RANGE, YOU CAN WALK THROUGH A BRILLIANT PRIMARY
FOREST WITH THE LAST REMAINING WA-NDOROBO OF
KENYA. SHE CAN ALSO INTRODUCE YOU TO THE ELEGANT
AND SOMETIMES DISTANT SAMBURU OF THE SURROUND-
ING DESERT. (BOX 82, NANYUKI, KENYA; TEL. 254-176-
22053)

A POSTSCRIPT

On your safari you will discover extraordinary needs throughout wild Africa. People struggling against gross economic inequities cry out for help. Animals threatened by poaching require advocates. Habitats on the verge of extinction must be protected.

In my experience, only the African Wildlife Foundation responds to all these needs effectively. In Tsavo and in the Serengeti it seeks to establish a realm of peaceful coexistence between wildlife and people. Tarangire has become the pride of Tanzania, in large part thanks to a cooperative venture between the government and AWF. Anti-poaching vehicles in the Selous are being serviced by a mobile repair vehicle supplied by AWF. Rhinos in Kenya, gorillas in Rwanda, chimpanzees at Gombe—all are benefiting from this small but efficient foundation.

Headquartered in Washington, D.C., and Nairobi, AWF was created nearly thirty years ago in response to African independence movements. Its first move was to help establish the College of African Wildlife Management in Mweka, Tanzania, in order to train indigenous peoples as replacements for departing expatriate game wardens. Today almost every national park in English-speaking Africa can boast Mweka graduates.

If your African safari has meant anything to you, I urge you to write or call the African Wildlife Foundation to see what you can do to help them sustain their valuable initiative.

The African Wildlife Foundation
1717 Massachusetts Avenue, NW,
Washington, DC 20036
Tel. 202-265-8394
or 800-344-TUSK

The African Wildlife Foundation
P.O.Box 48177
Nairobi, Kenya
Tel. 254-2-23235/331542

RHINO IN TSAVO EAST NATIONAL PARK, KENYA

A B O U T
T H E
A U T H O R

John Heminway has traveled extensively in Africa since childhood. After graduating from Princeton University, he wrote, directed, and produced many wildlife and anthropological documentaries for ABC Sports and Survival Anglia as well as much of the PBS award-winning series "The Brain" and "The Mind." He is currently the executive producer and host of the PBS "Travels" series. His books on Africa include The Imminent Rains and No Man's Land, published by Warner Books in 1989. Heminway is the chairman of the African Wildlife Foundation, and when not overseas he divides his time between New York and Montana.